TRADITIONAL

Daley
Bread

PENGUIN BOOKS

Penguin Books (NZ) Ltd, cnr Airborne and Rosedale Roads, Albany, Auckland 1310, New Zealand
Penguin Books Ltd, 27 Wrights Lane, London W8 5TZ, England
Penguin Putnam Inc, 375 Hudson Street, New York, NY 10014, United States
Penguin Books Australia Ltd, 487 Maroondah Highway, Ringwood, Australia 3134
Penguin Books Canada Ltd, 10 Alcorn Avenue, Toronto, Ontario, Canada M4V 3B2
Penguin Books (South Africa) Pty Ltd, 5 Watkins Street, Denver Ext 4, 2094, South Africa
Penguin Books India (P) Ltd, 11, Community Centre, Panchsheel Park, New Delhi 110 017, India

Penguin Books Ltd, Registered Offices: Harmondsworth, Middlesex, England

First published by Penguin Books (NZ) Ltd, 2000

1 3 5 7 9 10 8 6 4 2

Copyright © George Dale, 2000

Back cover photo of George by Craig Godley

Designed by Mary Egan
Typeset by Egan-Reid Ltd, Auckland
Illustrations by Dean Gray
Printed in Australia by Australian Print Group, Maryborough

www.penguin.com

TRADITIONAL

Daley Bread

A SELECTION OF CLASSIC RECIPES FOR YOUR BREAD MACHINE

George Dale

PENGUIN BOOKS

Acknowledgements

As man does not live by bread only my thanks are due to:

My wife Joy, who, faced with yet another bread invasion, stoically criticised only my spelling.

My daughter, Penny, whose skills as cook and librarian were invaluable in my research and recipe testing.

Kathie Hope, whose culinary skills once again helped with the 'fine tuning' of recipes.

Angela Hallam, who created order from the chaos of my copy.

Des Britten, who listened to my ideas and helped with advice on bread — both spiritual and temporal.

John Haldane, for his timely reminder that frumenty still exists and is alive and well in New Zealand today.

Inge Mayr and Hermann Schiftner, for sharing their knowledge of Austrian breadmaking — and their bread.

Penguin, my publishers, and their efficient and talented team at Auckland who put up with me — and still smile.

Thanks everybody.

Contents

Introduction

Tradition —

A custom or belief, based on usage and experience, passed down the generations, especially by word of mouth. Hence: 'traditional'.

Traditional Daley Bread, the fourth in my series of recipe books for the breadmaker, had its genesis back in 1988 during my early experiments converting handmade recipes for use in this latest piece of kitchen equipment.

The results were evaluated by a bunch of my colleagues each day. One bread stood out in the number of requests I received for a repeat performance. It was a plain barley loaf. There in the face of trendy, tasty, new recipes — the most requested bread was one made from a recipe that was probably new three thousand years ago!

The idea of making some of the world's oldest established breads, utilising the very latest technology, intrigued me. You have the result in your hand — a new recipe book with no new recipes — just a new approach utilising the knowledge our ancestors have passed down to us.

Dreamtime to Realtime —

Dreamtime is my term for the period for which there is no definite information, just intelligent guesswork about the ingredients and possible cooking methods thought to have been available. Archaeological findings show us that our ancestors were eating grain-based food, and cooking it, fifty thousand years ago! Exactly what form this bread took is a matter of conjecture. There are many books on this subject, but this is not one of them!

Realtime, as far as breadmaking is concerned, started with some of the earliest known records. The recipes in this book go back to about the same time, with one for a Sumerian flat bread of barley flavoured with sesame and onions from about 3000 BC. There is a recipe here also for an Egyptian Leavened Wheat Loaf, from about 1500 BC, and an English Manchet Bread recipe of about 1400 AD.

An amazing array of many thousands of breads has developed worldwide over the centuries. Here are sixty of them that you can create with your breadmaker, all especially converted from the original recipes for handmade bread. The renaissance of organic agriculture has made available a great number of ancient grains and seeds, untainted by pesticides or herbicides — the ideal ingredients to make traditional breads, full of flavour. A great many of the recipes have been adopted by other cultures over more recent times. The area of origin is given with each recipe along with regional variations.

The ingredients section will tell you what to use and what you can substitute. Along with many tips, there are directions for cooking whole grains and for creating your own leavens, starters and sourdoughs, just as our ancestors did before commercial yeasts were available. Special instructions appear in the recipes as appropriate.

In the machine section you will find out how to use your machine to get the best results from all the recipes. Here is new technology reversing the usual trend — not destroying but helping to re-create the skills of the past. It must be good!

Bon appétit!

George Dale

The Machines

For three-quarters of the recipes in this book only the Dough cycle of the breadmaker is used. If your machine is one of the few without a Dough programme, use the 'Basic' bread programme instead, and push the Stop button just before the final rise. Consult your machine instruction book because it should indicate when this is timed to start.

For the remaining recipes you may take a rest — the machine does all the work for you. But please study your machine instruction book. Successful breadmaking starts with your understanding of what your breadmaker does, and why, and when it does it.

The recipes in this book make use of the standard programmes —

- Basic (normal) Bake
- Rapid Bake (not for 'quick' or yeast-free breads)
- Wholemeal (Wholewheat) Bake
- French Bake
- Dough (only)

If your breadmaker controls are marked differently, consult the instruction and recipe book that came with your machine and compare similar recipe instructions.

Other hardware you will require in order to complete some of the recipes are:

- A rolling pin
- A sharp knife

- A baking tray (sheet)

- A standard loaf pan

- A 25 cm x $1\frac{1}{2}$ cm round baking tray

- A muffin tray — 75 mm diameter cups if possible

And, of course, a conventional oven.

After each use, when your breadmaker has cooled:

- Unplug the power cord.

- With a soft cloth or sponge, wipe inside to remove crumbs and other debris.

- Do not immerse any part of your breadmaker in water, or put water in it (except for the bread pan and kneading blade).

- Do not use any cleaner, solid or liquid. Just wipe inside and outside with a damp sponge. Do not lubricate any parts.

- Clean bread pan and kneading blade.

- After some use the oven interior and bread pan will develop a patina. This is quite normal.

- The most likely need for service will be replacement of the kneading shaft assembly in the bread pan.

- Have the machine checked by a service agent if any part is damaged or malfunctioning. Always get an estimate first for any repair.

The Ingredients

Bread is only as good as its ingredients. Use the freshest ingredients you can get and check the 'use by' dates. All the ingredients listed in the recipes can be obtained from most supermarkets and health food stores.

Wheat Flours

Either stoneground, unbleached white flour, or 'high grade' flour, or 'bread' flour is the basic white flour used in most recipes because of the high level of gluten-forming protein in this refined flour.

'Wholemeal' flour is similar to the above white refined flour, but has some germ and bran replaced after refining.

'Stoneground Wholemeal' flour is the complete milled grain still with the germ and bran.

> *Store flour in the original bag placed in an airtight container. (Wholemeal is best kept in the fridge, especially if it's 'Stoneground'.)*

Wheat Gluten Flour

This is added to wholemeal and other low protein flours to boost the gluten structure.

> *Store in an airtight container in the fridge.*

Other Grains

Rye, barley, oats, maize, buckwheat, millet, rice, etcetera, can all be used as described in the recipes.

Rising Agents

The recipes in this book use active dried yeast, leaven or sourdough starter. If Surebake, or other yeast with 'improvers', is substituted, add fifty percent more than the given recipe quantity.

🌾 *Never dissolve the yeast in water — just put it in dry.*

Some recipes use a leaven, or sourdough 'starter'. Three 'starters' are used in these recipes; they are simple to make and look after. Just follow the routine.

🌾 *All flours should be organic.*

🌾 *All water should be spring or bottled.*

🌾 *Containers should be non-metallic, clean, and able to hold twice the total volume you put in (bread dough can expand a lot).*

🌾 *Keep the starter in the refrigerator when not in use. Get it out in time to come up to room temperature before use.*

🌾 *Replace what you use by either:*

(a)   The same quantity — half flour, half water — stirred in, or,

(b)   The same quantity taken back from the 'risen' sponge before the rest of the recipe to be made up is added.

🌾 *Stir the starter from time to time. If a crust forms, stir it in. The starter should smell sour, not putrid. If it is 'off', throw it out and start again.*

For leaven or starter recipes, see page 7.

Rising Agents

1. Wheat Leaven

Mix: 1 cup wholemeal flour

1 cup water

$^{1}/_{2}$ teaspoon active dry yeast

Cover with a clean, dry linen teatowel, and leave in a warm place two to five days, until bubbles appear.

Add: 1 cup wholemeal flour

1 cup water

Cover as above and leave in a warm place until ferment starts again. It is now ready for use. Keep in refrigerator until required.

2. Rye Leaven

Follow the same process as for wheat leaven but use rye flour. Add to the first mix one tablespoon of wheat leaven (if you have some ready for use).

3. Sourdough Starter

Mix: 2 cups unbleached stoneground flour

2 cups water

1 teaspoon active dry yeast

2 teaspoons honey

Cover as for wheat leaven and leave in warm place for five days. Stir daily. It should be the consistency of thick mud! Stir in any liquid that rises to the top. Store in the refrigerator.

🌾   *Only use ingredients at room temperature because heat kills yeast and cold slows the action.*

Sugar

Use any form of sugar you like — white, brown, honey, treacle, maple sugar, maple syrup, rice syrup, molasses or golden syrup. Never use artificial chemical sweeteners. Yeast needs sugar to begin to work, but sugar also sweetens the bread and aids browning.

❦   When replacing solid sugars with liquid, reduce the liquid quantity in the recipe to compensate.

Salt

Use ordinary table salt, sea salt or kosher salt.

❦   Be careful with the quantities of yeast, sugar and salt. Together they form a very delicate balance in the formation of gluten, fermentation and carbon dioxide production. Adjustment of any of these ingredients, even by quite small amounts, will have a considerable effect on the volume and texture of the finished product.

❦   Beware of a salt content in other ingredients. Reduce salt ingredient to suit.

Fats

Use any you like — butter, shortening, lard, lecithin granules, sunflower oil, olive oil, vegetable oil or margarine. Fats add flavour and robustness to the bread. They also help it to keep better.

❦   If replacing lecithin granules with liquid lecithin, reduce recipe amount by half.

❦   When replacing solid fats with oil, reduce the liquid quantity in the recipe to compensate.

Liquid

Water, juices, yoghurt, soy milk or cow's milk are called for in the recipes. If you use dried milk instead of fresh milk you have to adjust the total liquid amount to compensate for the liquid in the milk.

> ❦ *A lot of recipes make a big issue of the temperature of the ingredients, especially the liquids. I recommend 18–20°C (room temperature) as okay for everything. In all the testing I have done in a great variety of machines the temperature has never been a problem.*

Eggs

When the recipe calls for eggs without specifying size, use whatever size of egg you have to hand. Beat the white and yolk together, place in your liquid measure and fill with the liquid ingredient up to the total liquid level required. Dried eggs, or egg replacer can be substituted.

Fruits

Dried, canned, frozen or fresh fruit can be used. Don't forget to adjust sugar, salt or liquid amounts slightly to allow for the liquid content of the fruit.

> ❦ *Always use at room temperature.*

Nuts

Any type of nuts can be substituted for those stated in the recipes.

> ❦ *Always chop nuts well. Don't use coarsely chopped ones.*

Herbs and Spices

All the herbs and spices used in the recipes in this book are of the dried, ready-prepared variety available from any supermarket. You can substitute fresh herbs but remember that dried herbs are more potent. If using fresh herbs, use at least double the quantity.

🌿 *The small airtight containers of dried herbs and spices should be stored in a cool, dark cupboard, away from light and heat.*

Dried Milk

The recipes in this book use dried 'whole' milk. You may substitute any other dried milk powder but you may need to adjust the fat content to compensate.

Cheese

Most cheeses can be substituted in the recipes by other similar textured cheese to your taste.

🌿 *Always check — if a cheese is 'extra' salty, reduce the salt in the recipe.*

🌿 *Make sure soft cheese such as feta, or cottage, is well drained before use.*

Essences and Flavourings

If using the liquid type, measure and include with the main liquid in the recipe.

🌿 *If flavouring with soy, or other sauces such as Worcestershire, reduce the salt in the recipe.*

Measuring

It is essential that all ingredients are measured accurately. All the recipes and tables of quantities in this book use the standard international metric volume measures in cups, tablespoons, and teaspoons.

🌿 *Beware the ubiquitous Australian tablespoon! It is 5 ml larger than the international metric standard.*

Scoop up the ingredients into your cup or spoon; don't pack them into the measure or tap the bottom to 'settle' them. Rather, let them fill the measure in a natural fashion without any pressure to get more in. This will produce a more accurate, consistent result.

Correct interpretation of all the recipes is most essential because automatic bread machines are designed to operate strictly within the fixed programmed cycle that you select when you push the button on the control panel. The machine only does what it is programmed to do with what you give it to work with.

     See Tables to help with equivalent measures.

Order of Ingredients
You must place the ingredients into the pan in the order laid down in the instruction book that came with your machine.

The recipes in this book are listed with the dry items first, liquid items last. Your machine's instruction book might ask you to do it the other way around. If so, just start at the bottom of the recipes in this book and work through to the top!

Programme
Use the programme cycle recommended in the recipes in this book.

Liquidity Check
Because environmental conditions can affect the moisture content of flour and other ingredients, you should check the mixture after the first five minutes of mixing or kneading. The dough should have a smooth 'satin' look, and be slightly sticky.

If too sticky or wet looking, add flour one tablespoon at a time. If dough looks stiff and 'tight', add water one tablespoon at a time.

Use a rubber spatula to scrape down ingredients sticking to the breadpan.

Storing Your Loaves

I find the most effective way is first to cool the loaf or rolls on a wire rack, then wrap tightly in foil and seal in a plastic bag before freezing. Most recipes in this book will still be good even after several weeks in the freezer. To use, remove the bag from the freezer and allow contents to thaw naturally (not in the microwave). Take the loaf or rolls from the bag, leaving the foil on, and warm them gently at 170°C in the oven: 20–30 minutes for a loaf or 10–15 minutes for rolls. Open the foil for the last five minutes (for a loaf) or two minutes (for rolls). Delicious!

The Recipes

If you have never handled yeast-risen dough before, this section will help remove the mystique. People have been working with dough for thousands of years. Don't be afraid of it — handle it and get used to the feel of this fascinating living material.

The Breadmaker section tells you how to use your machine with the recipes in this book. With step-by-step instructions and diagrams you will soon be producing your own traditional breads. First, just a little more information to help you on your way.

Refrigerating Dough

One or two recipes suggest storing the dough temporarily in a refrigerator as part of the process. This slows down the fermentation by reduction of temperature below 4°C to halt the yeast activity. To store:

- Place dough in a container big enough to allow for some expansion.
- Brush surface with oil or melted butter to prevent a crust forming.
- Cover tightly with plastic wrap and refrigerate.
- When ready to use, allow the dough to return to room temperature before proceeding.

Prepared Topping and Fillings

Many supermarkets and delicatessens carry a huge range of antipasto veggies, pizza toppings and pastes, and fruit and other fillings. Feel free to experiment as the fancy takes you. Be sure to check the liquid content before use, especially as some filling ingredients might become liquid during baking.

Recipe Sizes

All recipes in this book are standardized to the most popular $1^1/_2$ pound/750 gram loaf size. If you have to adjust this, use Table 4 to vary the recipe quantities by the correct proportions.

Finishing

The suggested fillings, shape or glaze in any recipe can be varied or altered to those suggested for any other similar recipe. Just mix and match as you fancy.

Farmer's Bread 'Burebrot' — Swiss Tyrol

Ingredients	Measure	
SPONGE		
Yeast	Teaspoon	3
Bread Flour	Cup	$1^1/_2$
Wholemeal Flour	Cup	1
Sugar	Teaspoon	1
Water	Cup	$1^1/_8$
DOUGH		
Rye Flour	Cup	$^1/_2$
Salt	Teaspoon	$1^1/_2$

- Place sponge ingredients in pan, select Dough cycle and press Start. After 10 minutes press Stop. Allow to rest for 90 minutes.

- Place remaining dough ingredients in pan with sponge. Select Wholewheat cycle and press Start again.

- Check liquidity of mixture.

- Remove bread from pan at end of Bake and cool on a rack.

Almond Baklava with Syrup — Iraq

For centuries baklava of one sort or another has been served at every occasion for celebration in Middle Eastern countries.

Finishing instructions for recipe on facing page:

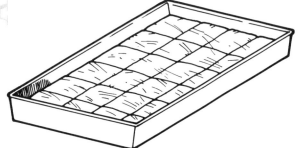

- Butter a 20 cm x 30 cm x 5 cm dish.

- Take a recipe quantity of 'sweet' laminated yeast dough (**see page 75**).

- Divide into two, roll out each piece 20 cm x 30 cm to fit dish.

- Place one piece to cover bottom of dish. Spread all of filling mixture to cover dough.
  Place second dough piece to cover filling.

- With a sharp blade score top dough in 5 cm squares.

- Brush on topping. Cover with a clean, dry linen teatowel and leave to rise in a warm place until doubled in volume.

- Bake as instructed.

Almond Baklava with Syrup – Iraq

Ingredients	Measure	
FILLING		
Chopped Almonds	Cup	2
Sugar	Cup	¹/₂
Cinnamon	Tablespoon	1
Allspice	Teaspoon	1
TOPPING		
Melted Butter	Tablespoon	4
SYRUP		
Sugar	Cup	6
Water	Cup	¹/₄
Lemon Juice	Teaspoon	1
Vanilla Extract	Teaspoon	¹/₂

- **See page 75 for sweet laminated yeast dough.**

- In a bowl combine nuts, sugar, cinnamon and allspice.

- **Refer to finishing instructions on facing page.**

- Place in pre-heated oven at 180°C for 35–40 minutes or until golden brown.

- When baklava is cooked, remove dish from oven and cool. Leave baklava in dish.

- Place all syrup ingredients in a saucepan, bring to boil, then simmer for 10 minutes. Cool completely.

- Pour all of syrup evenly over pastry.

- Cut through all layers and lift out squares to serve.

Arabic Pita Bread

Finishing instructions for recipe on facing page:

- Divide rested dough into six pieces.

- Roll pieces out to about 5 mm thick. Place on a cloth dusted with bran flakes.

- Cover with a clean, damp linen teatowel and leave to rise in a warm place for 20 minutes.

- Place on lightly greased or oiled tray and bake as instructed.

This pocket bread is enjoyed in many Middle Eastern countries.

Arabic Pita – 'Eish Baladi'

Ingredients	Measure	
Yeast	Teaspoon	3
Bread Flour	Cup	$^1/_2$
Wholemeal Flour	Cup	$1^1/_2$
Light Rye Flour	Cup	1
Sugar	Tablespoon	1
Salt	Teaspoon	1
Ground Cumin	Teaspoon	$^1/_2$
Oil	Tablespoon	1
Water	Cup	$1^1/_8$

- Place all dough ingredients in pan, select Dough cycle and press Start.

- Check liquidity of mixture.

- Remove dough at end of cycle and place on lightly floured bench. Cover with a clean, damp linen teatowel and allow to rest for 10 minutes.

- **Follow finishing instructions on facing page.**

- Cook in pre-heated oven at highest setting for 3–5 minutes.

- Remove pita breads from tray when baked and cool on a rack.

- Cut open along one side.

- Fill with hot savoury food or cold meat and chopped salad vegetables and herbs.

Austrian Rye Bread — Sourdough

In Central Europe, rye is the grain that grows best. The strong sour flavour of rye complements the many tasty foods served in Germany and Austria.

This recipe and the two following, especially converted for the breadmaker, are examples of the many rye grain breads produced for centuries by the skilled bakers of central Europe.

Austrian Rye Bread — Sourdough

Ingredients	Measure	
Yeast	Teaspoon	2¹/₂
Bread Flour	Cup	1
Rye Flour	Cup	2
Sourdough Starter	Cup	¹/₂
Sugar	Teaspoon	1
Salt	Teaspoon	2
Lecithin	Teaspoon	1
Caraway	Teaspoon	1
Coriander	Teaspoon	¹/₈
Aniseed	Teaspoon	¹/₈
Water	Cup	1

- **Use sourdough starter (page 7).**

- Place all dough ingredients in pan. Set Dark Crust, select Wholewheat cycle and press Start. Some breadmakers do not allow both Dark Crust and Wholewheat. For these, select Wholewheat.

- Check liquidity of mixture.

- Remove bread from pan at end of Bake and cool on a rack.

Herman's Bread — Rye

Ingredients	Measure	
Yeast	Teaspoon	$2^1/_2$
Bread Flour	Cup	$^3/_4$
Wholemeal Flour	Cup	$1^1/_2$
Rye Meal Flour	Cup	$1^1/_4$
Gluten Flour	Teaspoon	2
Sugar	Teaspoon	1
Salt	Teaspoon	2
Lecithin	Teaspoon	2
Caraway	Teaspoon	1
Coriander	Teaspoon	$^1/_8$
Aniseed	Teaspoon	$^1/_8$
Water	Cup	$1^1/_8$

- Place all dough ingredients in pan. Set Dark Crust, select Wholewheat cycle and press Start. Some breadmakers do not allow both Dark Crust and Wholewheat. For these, select Wholewheat.

- Check liquidity of mixture.

- Remove bread from pan at end of Bake and cool on a rack.

Bavarian Rye Bread

Ingredients	Measure	
Yeast	Teaspoon	3
Bread Flour	Cup	2
Rye Meal Flour	Cup	1
Black Treacle	Tablespoon	1
Salt	Teaspoon	1
Shortening	Tablespoon	1
Caraway	Teaspoon	1$^{1}/_{2}$
Water	Cup	1$^{1}/_{8}$

🌾 Place all dough ingredients in pan. Set Dark Crust, select Wholewheat cycle and press Start. Some breadmakers do not allow both Dark Crust and Wholewheat. For these, select Wholewheat.

🌾 Check liquidity of mixture.

🌾 Remove bread from pan at end of Bake and cool on a rack.

Bagels

'Bagel' is a Yiddish word for a chewy bread roll. It migrated with the Jews through the Middle East, Balkans, Russia and the whole of Europe — thence to North America where it became the standby of the delicatessen trade. And now it is international.

A feature of the Bar Mitzvah and many other Jewish celebrations are bagels with cream cheese and lox, or other smoked fish, usually served with thinly sliced onion, tomato and cucumber.

'Lox' — from the Yiddish 'laks' (smoked salmon).

These finishing instructions are for the bagel recipes on pages 26–29:

🌾   When rested, roll dough into a 25 cm long log shape.

🌾   Cut into 10 pieces with sharp knife.

🌾   Roll each piece into a firm ball.

🌾   Slightly flatten ball and push a floured finger through to form a ring. Increase diameter of hole by stretching gently to approximately 6–7 cm. (This will reduce as dough rises.)

🌾   Place on oiled baking tray to rise 10–20 minutes.

🌾   In a suitable sized pan, bring poaching water and sugar to boil. Turn down to simmer gently.

🌾   Place each bagel in boiling water for 30 seconds. Drain on a rack and return to baking tray.

🌾   Mix glaze. Brush glaze on each bagel and sprinkle with topping.

🌾   Bake as instructed.

The Classic Bagel

Ingredients	Measure	
DOUGH		
Yeast	Teaspoon	2
Bread Flour	Cup	3
Gluten Flour	Tablespoon	1
Sugar (Brown)	Tablespoon	1¹/₂
Salt (Kosher)	Teaspoon	1¹/₂
Olive Oil	Tablespoon	1
Water	Cup	1
POACHING		
Water	Cup	8
Sugar	Tablespoon	2
GLAZE		
Egg		1
Water	Tablespoon	1
TOPPING		
Sesame Seed	As required	

- Place all dough ingredients in pan, select Dough cycle and press Start.

- Check liquidity of mixture.

- Remove dough at end of cycle and place on lightly floured bench. Cover with a clean, damp linen teatowel and allow to rest for 10 minutes.

- **Follow finishing instructions on page 25.**

- Cook in pre-heated oven at 200°C for 20–25 minutes.

- Remove bagels from tray when baked and cool on a rack.

Ingredients	Measure	
DOUGH		
Yeast	Teaspoon	$2^1/_2$
Bread Flour	Cup	$1^1/_2$
Wholemeal Flour	Cup	$1^1/_4$
Wheatgerm	Tablespoon	4
Gluten Flour	Tablespoon	2
Honey	Tablespoon	1
Salt (Kosher)	Teaspoon	$1^1/_2$
Water	Cup	1
POACHING		
Water	Cup	8
GLAZE		
Egg		1
Water	Tablespoon	1

Place all dough ingredients in pan, select Dough cycle and press Start.

Check liquidity of mixture.

Remove dough at end of cycle and place on lightly floured bench. Cover with a clean, damp linen teatowel and allow to rest for 10 minutes.

Follow finishing instructions on page 25.

Cook in pre-heated oven at 200°C for 20–25 minutes.

Remove bagels from tray when baked and cool on a rack.

Onion Bagels

Ingredients	Measure	
DOUGH		
Yeast	Teaspoon	2
Bread Flour	Cup	3
Gluten Flour	Tablespoon	1
Sugar	Tablespoon	1½
Salt (Kosher)	Teaspoon	1½
Butter	Tablespoon	1½
Water	Cup	1
Minced Onion	Cup	1
POACHING		
Water	Cup	8
Sugar	Tablespoon	1
GLAZE		
Egg		1
Water	Tablespoon	1

- Place first seven dough ingredients in pan, select Dough cycle and press Start.

- Check liquidity of mixture.

- Place minced onion in pan when 'beep' sounds, or 10 minutes from end of final kneading.

- Remove dough at end of cycle and place on lightly floured bench. Cover with a clean, damp linen teatowel and allow to rest for 10 minutes.

- **Follow finishing instructions on page 25.**

- Cook in pre-heated oven at 200°C for 20–25 minutes.

- Remove bagels from tray when baked and cool on a rack.

Cinnamon Raisin Bagels

Ingredients	Measure	
DOUGH		
Yeast	Teaspoon	2
Bread Flour	Cup	3
Gluten Flour	Tablespoon	1
Sugar (Brown)	Tablespoon	1$^1/_2$
Salt (Kosher)	Teaspoon	1$^1/_2$
Butter (Unsalted)	Tablespoon	1
Water	Cup	1
Ground Cinnamon	Teaspoon	2
Raisins	Cup	$^3/_4$
POACHING		
Water	Cup	8
Sugar	Tablespoon	2
GLAZE		
Egg		1
Water	Tablespoon	1

- Place first seven dough ingredients in pan, select Dough cycle and press Start.

- Check liquidity of mixture.

- Place remaining dough ingredients in pan when 'beep' sounds, or 10 minutes from end of final kneading.

- Remove dough at end of cycle and place on lightly floured bench. Cover with a clean, damp linen teatowel and allow to rest for 10 minutes.

- **Follow finishing instructions on page 25.**

- Cook in pre-heated oven at 200°C for 20–25 minutes.

- Remove bagels from tray when baked and cool on a rack.

Barley Honey Bread — Roman

The Roman Legions had been in Britain about three hundred years when this fairly dense bread was first made. The Romans would have used a leaven instead of yeast, and milk instead of milk powder, but the result would have been the same.

The Romans kept almost all the British wheat production for themselves. The Brits had to make do with barley and oats. Later, the Romans took to barley bread.

Finishing instructions for recipe on facing page:

- Divide rested dough into two pieces. Roll each into a ball, then press lightly into a 25 cm circle.

- Place both flat breads onto a greased or oiled baking tray. Cover with a clean, damp linen teatowel and leave to rise for 20–30 minutes in a warm place.

- Brush tops with milk.

- Bake as directed.

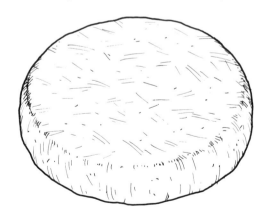

Barley Honey Bread — Roman

Ingredients	Measure	
DOUGH		
Yeast	Teaspoon	3
Bread Flour	Cup	2
Barley Flour	Cup	1
Honey	Tablespoon	2
Olive Oil	Tablespoon	1
Salt	Teaspoon	1
Milk Powder	Tablespoon	2
Water	Cup	1$\frac{1}{8}$
TOPPING		
Milk	Tablespoon	2

- Place all dough ingredients in pan, select Dough cycle and press Start.

- Check liquidity of mixture.

- Remove dough at end of cycle and place on lightly floured bench. Allow to rest for 30 minutes.

- **Follow finishing instructions on facing page.**

- Cook in pre-heated oven at 190°C for 35–45 minutes.

- Remove bread from tray at end of Bake and cool on a rack.

Barley Onion Flatbread — Sumerian

Barley, once the major grain for breadmaking, is now chiefly used for brewer's malt. The Sumerians were also ahead here. They are said to have been producing eight different types of barley beer by about 2800 BC!

Barley alone makes a very dense bread. Mixed with wheat (which was available in the form of emmer), the bread is a little lighter.

Finishing instructions for recipe on facing page:

- Divide rested dough into two.

- Roll each into a ball. Flatten each out to a circle about 22 cm diameter. Place on floured cloth to rise in a warm place for 60 minutes until well risen.

- Brush tops with water and sprinkle on sesame seed.

- Bake as instructed.

Barley Onion Flatbread — Sumerian

Ingredients	Measure	
SPONGE		
Yeast	Teaspoon	1
Barley Flour	Cup	$^1/_2$
Wholemeal Flour	Cup	$1^1/_2$
Water	Cup	$1^1/_8$
DOUGH		
Salt	Teaspoon	$^1/_2$
Barley Flour	Cup	1
Finely Chopped Onion	Cup	1
TOPPING		
Water	Tablespoon	2
Sesame Seed	Tablespoon	1

- Place sponge ingredients in pan, select Dough cycle and press Start. After 10 minutes press Stop. Allow to rest 4 hours.

- Place remaining dough ingredients in pan with sponge, select Dough cycle again and press Start.

- Check liquidity of mixture.

- Remove dough at end of cycle and place on lightly floured bench. Allow to rest for 60 minutes in a warm place.

- **Follow finishing instructions on facing page.**

- Cook on pre-heated griddle at 200°C for 20–25 minutes.

- Remove bread from griddle when baked and cool on a rack.

Buckwheat Börek — Turkish

Börek, or Bourekas — little baked dough cases filled with an assortment of tasty fillings — are found in all Middle Eastern, and East European countries. They have developed over the years as a convenient snack food for travellers.

Finishing instructions for recipes on pages 35–37:

- Take a recipe quantity of plain laminated yeast dough, (**see page 74**). Divide into two and roll out each piece to 20 cm x 40 cm. Cut each into eight 10 cm x 10 cm squares.

- Place 3 tablespoons of filling in centre of each square. Bring opposite corners together, to enclose filling in triangle-shaped case and seal edges.

- Place on oiled or greased baking tray in a warm place, cover with a clean, damp linen teatowel and leave until doubled in volume.

- Brush with topping and sprinkle with seeds.

- Bake as instructed.

Buckwheat Börek — Turkish

Ingredients	Measure	
FILLING		
Buckwheat (Kasha), cooked	Cup	1¹/₂
Egg (lightly beaten)		1
Oil	Tablespoon	3
Chopped Onion	Cup	³/₄
Chopped Mushroom	Cup	³/₄
Salt	To taste	
Pepper	To taste	
Chopped Almonds	Tablespoon	2
Egg (lightly beaten)		1
TOPPING		
Egg (beaten with pinch of salt)		1

- **See page 74 for plain laminated yeast dough recipe.**

- **See page 60 to cook buckwheat.**

- In a bowl mix cooked buckwheat with first beaten egg until all grains are coated.

- Heat oil in a pan. Sauté onions and mushrooms until soft. Add salt and pepper. Stir well.

- Remove from heat. Stir in buckwheat mixture and nuts.

- Transfer to a bowl and stir in second beaten egg. Season further as required. Cool completely.

- **Refer to facing page for finishing instructions.**

- Cook in pre-heated oven at 190°C for 20–25 minutes or until golden brown.

- Remove börek from tray when baked and cool on a rack.

Cheese Bourekas — Israeli

Ingredients	Measure	
FILLING		
Cottage Cheese (low fat)	Cup	$^1/_2$
Grated Kashkaval, or Swiss, or Cheddar Cheese	Cup	2
Egg (lightly beaten)		2
Chopped Spring Onions	Cup	$^1/_2$
Salt	To taste	
Pepper	To taste	
TOPPING		
Melted Butter	Tablespoon	2
Sesame Seed	Tablespoon	1

- **See page 74 for plain laminated yeast dough recipe.**

- Gently press cottage cheese in a strainer and leave for 10 minutes to remove excess moisture.

- In a bowl mix together eggs, both cheeses and onions. Add pepper and salt to taste.

- **Refer to page 34 for finishing instructions.**

- Cook in pre-heated oven at 180°C for 20–25 minutes or until golden brown.

- Remove bourekas from tray when done and cool on a rack.

Spinach Bourekas — Syrian

Ingredients	Measure	
FILLING		
Cooked Chopped Spinach	Cup	2
Egg (lightly beaten)		2
Grated Swiss Cheese	Cup	$^1/_2$
Finely Chopped Onion	Cup	$^1/_2$
Pepper	To taste	
Salt	To taste	
Nutmeg	To taste	
TOPPING		
Melted Butter	Tablespoon	2
Sesame or Poppy Seeds	Tablespoon	1

- **See page 74 for plain laminated yeast dough recipe.**

- Press chopped spinach in a strainer to remove excess moisture.

- In a bowl mix together eggs, spinach, cheese and onion. Add pepper, salt and nutmeg to taste.

- **Refer to page 34 for finishing instructions.**

- Cook in pre-heated oven at 180°c for 25–30 minutes, or until golden brown.

- Remove bourekas from tray when done and cool on a rack.

Cherry Pie — Romanian

The Romanians are fully justified in their love of the big juicy cherries grown in their country. Most people, when making their bread, will always divert a portion of the dough to make this delicious sweet treat.

Finishing instructions for recipe on facing page:

- Divide rested dough into two pieces. Roll one piece to 35 cm diameter and one to 28 cm diameter.

- Butter a 25 cm diameter deep pie dish and line with larger piece.

- Mix together all filling ingredients and put in lined dish. Cover with remaining dough piece, moisten dough edges and seal. Cover with a clean, damp linen teatowel and leave to rise in a warm place for 15–30 minutes.

- Brush with glaze.

- Bake as instructed.

Cherry Pie — Romanian

Ingredients	Measure	
DOUGH		
Yeast	Teaspoon	2^1/$_2$
Bread Flour	Cup	3
Sugar	Tablespoon	2
Salt	Teaspoon	^{1}/$_2$
Milk Powder	Tablespoon	2
Egg (measure with water)		1
Water	Cup	1^1/$_8$
FILLING		
Chopped Walnuts	Cup	^{1}/$_2$
Pitted Cherries	Cup	4
Soft Breadcrumbs	Cup	1
Castor Sugar	Cup	^{1}/$_2$
GLAZE		
Melted Butter	Tablespoon	1
TOPPING		
Icing Sugar	Tablespoon	1

- Place all dough ingredients in pan, select Dough cycle and press Start.

- Check liquidity of mixture.

- Remove dough at end of cycle, place on lightly floured bench and allow to rest for 10 minutes.

- **Follow finishing instructions on facing page.**

- Cook in pre-heated oven at 190°C for 35–40 minutes.

- Remove pie from dish as soon as possible and cool on a rack.

- Sprinkle top with icing sugar.

Chicken and Apricot Pie — Greek

This pie's tasty filling is found in many guises throughout the Greek Islands. Here is the filling at its best, as originally made, enclosed in a laminated yeast dough.

Finishing instructions for recipe on facing page:

- Take half the plain laminated dough recipe amount from **page 74**. Divide in two and roll each piece into a ball. Roll out each ball into a 28 cm diameter disc.

- Brush a 25 cm round deep pie dish with melted butter. Line dish with the first dough piece. Spoon in the chicken mixture.

- Cover with remaining second dough piece. Moisten dough edges and seal. Brush on remaining butter.

- Bake as instructed.

Chicken and Apricot Pie — Greek

Ingredients	Measure	
FILLING		
Chopped Onion	Cup	1/2
Minced Chicken	Cup	1 1/2
Melted Butter	Tablespoon	4
Chopped Apricots	Cup	1/4
Chopped Almonds	Cup	1/4
Cooked Bulgur Wheat	Cup	1/2
Ground Cinnamon	Teaspoon	1
Ground Allspice	Teaspoon	1/2
Plain Yoghurt	Cup	1/4
Chopped Chives	Tablespoon	1
Chopped Parsley	Tablespoon	2
Salt	To taste	
Pepper	To taste	

- **See page 74 for plain laminated yeast dough recipe.**

- **See page 60 to cook bulgur wheat.**

- In a frying pan, gently cook onion and chicken in 2 tablespoons of butter until golden.

- Stir in apricots, almonds and wheat. Cook for a further 2 minutes.

- Remove from heat. Stir in cinnamon, allspice, yoghurt, chives and parsley. Season to taste with salt and pepper.

- **Refer to facing page for finishing instructions.**

- Place in pre-heated oven at 200°C for 30–40 minutes until golden brown.

Churek — Armenian Flat Bread

This delicious chewy bread is a staple of the Armenian table. It's enjoyed at every meal and consumed in vast quantities.

Finishing instructions for recipe on facing page:

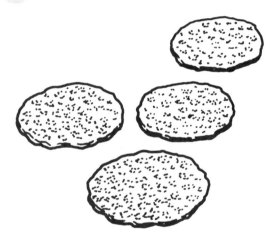

- Divide rested dough into five pieces. Roll each piece into a ball, then flatten balls into circles as thin as possible. Cover with a clean, damp linen teatowel until doubled in volume.

- Place on oiled or greased baking tray. Brush lightly with water and sprinkle with seeds.

- Bake as instructed.

Churek — Armenian Flat Bread

Ingredients	Measure	
DOUGH		
Yeast	Teaspoon	2¹/₂
Bread Flour	Cup	3
Sugar	Tablespoon	¹/₂
Salt	Teaspoon	1
Butter	Tablespoon	2
Water	Cup	1¹/₈
TOPPING		
Warm Water	Tablespoon	2
Sesame Seed	Tablespoon	1

- Place all dough ingredients in pan, select Dough cycle and press Start.

- Check liquidity of mixture.

- Remove dough at end of cycle and place on lightly floured bench. Allow to rest for 10 minutes.

- **Follow finishing instructions on facing page.**

- Cook in pre-heated oven at 200°C for 20–25 minutes until golden.

- Remove baked flatbreads from tray and place on a rack to cool.

Country Milk Rolls — USA

These small tender rolls enriched with milk and sprinkled with poppy seeds have appeared all over the world. This recipe came to me from the USA.

Finishing instructions for recipe on facing page:

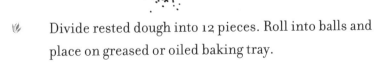

- Divide rested dough into 12 pieces. Roll into balls and place on greased or oiled baking tray.

- Cover with a clean, damp linen teatowel and leave to rise in a warm place until doubled in volume.

- Brush each roll with beaten egg glaze and sprinkle with poppy seed.

- Bake as instructed.

This dough may be fashioned into many of the other roll shapes illustrated in this book.

Country Milk Rolls — USA

Ingredients	Measure	
DOUGH		
Yeast	Teaspoon	2$^1/_2$
Bread Flour	Cup	3
Milk Powder	Tablespoon	4
Sugar	Teaspoon	1
Salt	Teaspoon	$^1/_4$
Water	Cup	1$^1/_8$
TOPPING		
Egg (beaten)		1
Poppy Seed	Tablespoon	2

🌾 Place all dough ingredients in pan, select Dough cycle and press Start.

🌾 Check liquidity of mixture.

🌾 Remove dough at end of cycle and place on lightly floured bench. Allow to rest for 10 minutes.

🌾 **Follow finishing instructions on facing page.**

🌾 Cook in pre-heated oven at 180°C for approximately 15–20 minutes.

🌾 Remove rolls from tray when baked and cool on a rack.

Country Wholewheat — USA

This tasty chewy bread, like some other breads in this book, uses a 'sponge' to start the yeast action before the salt is added. This allows the yeast and gluten to develop quickly before the salt exerts its controlling influence.

Finishing instructions for recipe on facing page:

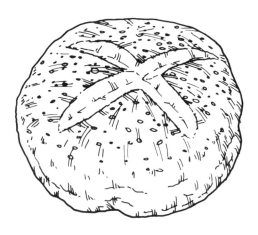

- Roll rested dough into a smooth ball by tucking all loose ends underneath. Place on greased or oiled baking tray and slightly flatten top. Cover with a clean, damp linen teatowel and leave to rise in a warm place for about 20 minutes.

- Slash top with two cuts, brush with water and sprinkle with pumpkin seeds.

- Bake as instructed.

Country Wholewheat — USA

Ingredients	Measure	
SPONGE		
Yeast	Teaspoon	2$^1/_2$
Wholemeal Flour	Cup	2
Molasses	Tablespoon	2
Milk Powder	Tablespoon	4
Water	Cup	1$^1/_8$
DOUGH		
Wholemeal Flour	Cup	1
Butter	Tablespoon	2
Salt	Teaspoon	$^1/_2$
TOPPING		
Water	Tablespoon	1
Pumpkin Seeds	Tablespoon	1

❧ Place sponge ingredients in pan, select Dough cycle and press Start. After 10 minutes press Stop. Allow to rest for 60 minutes.

❧ Place remaining dough ingredients in pan with sponge, select Dough cycle again and press Start.

❧ Check liquidity of mixture.

❧ Remove dough at end of cycle and place on lightly floured bench. Cover with a clean, damp linen teatowel and allow to rest for 35 minutes.

❧ **Follow finishing instructions on facing page.**

❧ Cook in pre-heated oven at 180°C for about 60 minutes.

❧ Remove from tray and cool on a rack.

Cypriot Cheese Breads

Enjoyed by both the Greek and Turkish communities, these little filled breads are a well-established fact of life in Cyprus. Ideally halumi cheese is used, but feta is more readily available.

Finishing instructions for recipe on facing page:

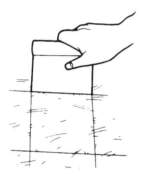

- Divide rested dough into six pieces and roll each piece into a 20 cm x 20 cm square.

- Divide the filling into six and pile into centre of each dough piece.

- Bring dough corners together over filling and pinch to seal.

- Place on greased or oiled baking tray seam downwards, coat with oil and leave to rise in a warm place until doubled in volume.

- Bake as instructed.

Cypriot Cheese Breads

Ingredients	Measure	
DOUGH		
Yeast	Teaspoon	2¹/₂
Bread Flour	Cup	1¹/₂
Wholemeal Flour	Cup	1¹/₂
Sugar	Tablespoon	1
Salt	Teaspoon	1
Water	Cup	1¹/₈
FILLING		
Crumbled Feta Cheese	Cup	2
Pitted Sliced Olives	Cup	1
TOPPING		
Olive Oil	Tablespoon	2

- Place all dough ingredients in pan, select Dough cycle and press Start.

- Check liquidity of mixture.

- Remove dough at end of cycle and place on lightly floured bench. Cover with a clean, damp linen teatowel and allow to rest for 10 minutes.

- **Follow finishing instructions on facing page.**

- Cook in pre-heated oven at 230°C for 10–15 minutes.

- Remove baked breads from tray and cool on a rack.

Doughnuts

Fluffy balls of dough, deep fried and dredged in sugar are now almost universal. Known as 'krapfen' in Germany, 'boules' in France and 'soofganiyot' in Israel, they are just another example of different cultures developing yeast-leavened bread dough in similar ways.

The variations of fillings (jam, fruit etc) and toppings (icing, spices, syrups etc) are seemingly endless — the choice is yours. Here they are plain, the only universal recipe!

Finishing instructions for recipe on facing page:

- Divide rested dough into 12–16 pieces.

- Roll each piece into a smooth ball. Place on greased or oiled baking tray. Cover with a clean, damp linen teatowel and leave to rise in a warm place for 15–30 minutes.

- Deep fry as instructed, a few at a time. Do not overcrowd.

- When drained, dredge in sugar and cinnamon.

Ingredients	Measure	
DOUGH		
Yeast	Teaspoon	2¹/₂
Bread Flour	Cup	3
Sugar	Tablespoon	1¹/₂
Salt	Teaspoon	¹/₂
Egg (measure with water)		1
Milk Powder	Tablespoon	2
Water	Cup	1¹/₈
TOPPING		
Castor Sugar	Tablespoon	2
Cinnamon	Teaspoon	1

- Place all dough ingredients in pan, select Dough cycle and press Start.

- Check liquidity of mixture.

- Remove dough at end of cycle and place on lightly floured bench. Cover with a clean, damp linen teatowel and allow to rest in a warm place for 10 minutes.

- **Follow finishing instructions on facing page.**

- Pre-heat oil for deep fryer. Fry at 180°C for 5–10 minutes until golden.

- Remove to drain on a rack lined with kitchen paper.

Easter Bread — Greek

In Greece, Easter celebrations are very important. This bread is one made especially for the occasion. It is sometimes accompanied by decorated eggs.

Finishing instructions for recipe on facing page:

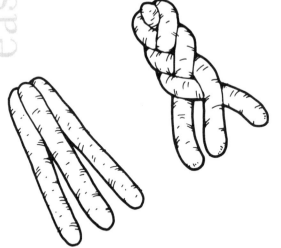

- Divide rested dough into three, and roll each piece into a 30 cm long sausage shape.

- Plait the three pieces together as shown and tuck ends under. Place on greased or oiled baking tray. Cover with a clean, damp linen teatowel and leave to rise in a warm place until doubled in volume.

- Brush with egg white and sprinkle with slivered almonds.

- Bake as instructed.

Easter Bread — Greek

Ingredients	Measure	
SPONGE		
Yeast	Teaspoon	$2^1/_2$
Bread Flour	Cup	1
Milk Powder	Tablespoon	1
Water	Cup	$^3/_4$
DOUGH		
Bread Flour	Cup	2
Sugar	Tablespoon	$^1/_2$
Butter	Tablespoon	2
Brandy	Tablespoon	1
Caraway Seed	Teaspoon	$^1/_2$
Egg (whole)	Beaten	1
Egg (yolk)	together	1
Water	Cup	$^1/_4$
TOPPING		
Egg (white)	Beaten	1
Slivered Almonds	Cup	$^1/_4$

- Place sponge ingredients in pan, select Dough cycle and press Start. After 10 minutes press Stop. Allow to rest for 60 minutes.

- Place all dough ingredients in pan with sponge, select Dough cycle and press Start again.

- Check liquidity of mixture.

- Remove dough at end of cycle and place on lightly floured bench. Cover with a clean, damp linen teatowel and allow to rest in a warm place for 10 minutes.

- **Follow finishing instructions on facing page.**

- Cook in pre-heated oven at 180°C for 60 minutes.

- Remove bread from tray when baked and cool on a rack.

English Muffins — Original

From the fifteenth to the early twentieth century the muffin man was a familiar sight in English towns and cities. This trade was by 'old' soldiers making a living after army service.

Finishing instructions for recipe on facing page:

- Roll out rested dough to approximately 1 cm thickness. Cut into rounds with 8 cm cutter. Place on floured cloth, cover with a clean, dry linen teatowel and leave to rise 20–30 minutes in a warm place. Dust tops with flour.

- Cook as instructed.

The 'correct' way to eat muffins is to pull the top from the bottom with the fingers (do not cut!), toast slowly, and butter well.

English Muffins — Original

Ingredients	Measure	
Yeast	Teaspoon	2 ¹/₂
Bread Flour	Cup	3
Sugar	Teaspoon	1
Salt	Teaspoon	1
Shortening	Tablespoon	1
Water	Cup	1¹/₈

- Place all dough ingredients in pan, select Dough cycle and press Start.

- Check liquidity of mixture.

- Remove dough at end of cycle and place on lightly floured bench. Cover with a clean, dry linen teatowel and allow to rest for 10 minutes.

- **Follow finishing instructions on facing page.**

- Cook on pre-heated griddle or pan at 175°C for 5–6 minutes each side.

- Remove muffins from griddle when cooked and cool on a rack.

Cornbread — Italian

Ingredients	Measure	
Yeast	Teaspoon	3
Bread Flour	Cup	$1^1/_2$
Cornmeal (Polenta)	Cup	$1^1/_2$
Salt	Teaspoon	$^1/_2$
Olive Oil	Tablespoon	1
Water	Cup	$1^1/_8$

- Place all dough ingredients in pan, select Wholemeal cycle and press Start.

- Check liquidity of mixture.

- Remove bread from pan at end of Bake and cool on a rack.

Wheat-based Bread Variations — English

Ingredients	Measure	
Yeast	Teaspoon	3
Bread Flour	Cup	2
Barley Flour *	Cup	1
Salt	Teaspoon	$1/2$
Water	Cup	$1^1/_8$

* Note: Buckwheat Flour, Millet Flour and Oat Flour can all be used instead of the Barley Flour in this recipe.

- Place all dough ingredients in pan, select Wholemeal cycle and press Start.
- Check liquidity of mixture.
- Remove bread from pan at end of bake and cool on a rack.

You can make these flours from whole grains in your kitchen blender.

Frumenty

This is where it all began, back in the 'dreamtime' period of grain food preparation, when seeds and grains were soaked (later boiled) in water to make them edible.

From this process to the bread we eat today development has been huge, but we still return to the original process. Different cultures have over the centuries used the grain they could grow best — oats for porridge (Celtic), buckwheat for kasha (Slav), maize for hominy (Algonquian) and wheat for frumenty (English).

The word 'frumenty' is medieval English, but the food itself has been traced back to the Old English and many thousands of years beyond.

On medieval feast days, frumenty was elaborate fare — wheat grains crushed, boiled in milk or water, enriched with eggs, sweetened with honey, coloured with saffron, and spiced. An English recipe book published in 1655 said that frumenty should be eaten cold with roasted red deer.

Many people today still eat it as a breakfast food — move over Mr Kellogg!!

The bread on the next page is good too.

Frumenty (Cooked Grain) Bread
— English

Ingredients	Measure	
DOUGH		
Yeast	Teaspoon	3
Wholemeal Flour	Cup	1
Bread Flour	Cup	$1^1/_2$
Cooked Buckwheat *	Cup	$^1/_2$
Sugar	Tablespoon	1
Salt	Teaspoon	$^1/_2$
Shortening	Tablespoon	2
Water	Cup	$1^1/_8$
Raisins	Cup	$^1/_2$

* Note: Other cooked grains can be used instead of buckwheat in this recipe. **See page 60.**

- Place first eight dough ingredients in pan, select Wholemeal cycle and press Start.

- Check liquidity of mixture.

- Place raisins in pan when 'beep' sounds, or 10 minutes from end of final kneading.

- Remove bread from pan at end of Bake and cool on a rack.

Cooking Whole Grains

For each cup of whole, uncooked, unsalted, clean grain	Fresh Water	Simmering Time	Approximate Yield
Buckwheat (Kasha)	2 Cups	10 Minutes	3$\frac{1}{2}$ Cups
Bulgur	2 Cups	15 Minutes	2$\frac{1}{2}$ Cups
Cornmeal	3$\frac{1}{2}$ Cups	25 Minutes	4 Cups
Millet	1$\frac{3}{4}$ Cups	30 Minutes	2$\frac{1}{2}$ Cups
Rice (White)	2 Cups	20 Minutes	3 Cups
Rice (Brown)	2 Cups	60 Minutes	3 Cups
Wheat	2$\frac{1}{4}$ Cups	60 Minutes	3 Cups

✹ In a large heavy pan bring water to a full boil. Stir in the grain, adjust to simmer, cover and cook for time given. Do not lift lid. The grain is ready when all liquid has been absorbed and surface of contents is dotted with steam holes.

✹ Use in recipes requiring whole (cooked) grains.

Babka — Polish 'Grandmother' Cake

Ingredients	Measure	
DOUGH		
Yeast	Teaspoon	2
Bread Flour	Cup	3
Castor Sugar	Tablespoon	2
Salt	Teaspoon	1/2
Butter	Tablespoon	2
Milk Powder	Tablespoon	2
Egg Yolks		3
Orange Zest	Teaspoon	2
Water	Cup	1
Sultanas	Cup	1
GLAZE		
Warmed Honey	Tablespoon	4

- Place first nine dough ingredients in pan, select Basic cycle and press Start.

- Check liquidity of mixture.

- Place sultanas in pan when 'beep' sounds or 10 minutes from end of final kneading.

- Remove bread from pan at end of Bake and cool on a rack.

- Brush glaze on when cake is cool.

Honey Challah — For Rosh Hashanah

Plaited challah are usual for the Sabbath. This honey-sweet spiral is a Jewish New Year special.

The Jewish New Year coincides with the northern hemisphere honey harvest. Two other European honey breads (**see pages 64 and 65**) are usually made at the same time of the year.

Finishing instructions for recipe on facing page:

- Roll rested dough into a rope about 60 cm long.

- Form rope into a spiral as shown and tuck end under.

- Place on greased or oiled baking tray.

- Cover with a clean, damp linen teatowel and leave to rise in a warm place until almost double in volume.

- Brush with glaze and sprinkle with seeds.

- Bake as instructed.

Honey Challah — For Rosh Hashanah

Ingredients	Measure	
DOUGH		
Yeast	Teaspoon	2
Bread Flour	Cup	3
Honey	Tablespoon	4
Salt (Kosher)	Teaspoon	1
Egg (measure with water)		2
Butter	Tablespoon	2
Water	Cup	1¹/₈
Raisins	Cup	¹/₂
GLAZE		
Egg (beaten)		1
Sesame Seed	Teaspoon	2

🌿 Place first seven dough ingredients in pan, select Dough cycle and press Start.

🌿 Check liquidity of mixture.

🌿 Place raisins in pan when 'beep' sounds, or 10 minutes from end of final kneading.

🌿 Remove dough at end of cycle and place on lightly floured bench. Cover with a clean, damp linen teatowel and allow to rest in a warm place for 10 minutes.

🌿 **Follow finishing instructions on facing page.**

🌿 Cook in pre-heated oven at 180°c for 25–35 minutes.

🌿 Remove challah from tray when baked and cool on a rack.

Wholemeal Honey Bread — Alsace

Ingredients	Measure	
Yeast	Teaspoon	3
Wholemeal Flour	Cup	3
Honey	Tablespoon	4
Salt	Teaspoon	¹/₂
Milk Powder	Tablespoon	4
Butter	Tablespoon	1
Water	Cup	1

- Place all dough ingredients in pan, select Wholewheat cycle and press Start.

- Check liquidity of mixture.

- Remove bread from pan at end of Bake and cool on a rack.

Swiss Honey Bread

Ingredients	Measure	
Yeast	Teaspoon	2¹/₂
Bread Flour	Cup	1¹/₂
Wholemeal Flour	Cup	1¹/₂
Dark Honey	Tablespoon	4
Salt	Teaspoon	1
Olive Oil	Tablespoon	2
Milk Powder	Tablespoon	2
Water	Cup	1

🌾 Place all dough ingredients in pan, select Wholewheat cycle and press Start.

🌾 Check liquidity of mixture.

🌾 Remove bread from pan at end of Bake and cool on a rack.

Hot Cross Buns

Long before Christianity came to Europe, the pagan gods and goddesses of the sun, earth, and fertility were celebrated during the spring equinox by the baking of breads decorated with their symbols.

The new faith adopted the food, and the fertility symbols changed to crosses, thus becoming part of the Easter celebrations.

Finishing instructions for recipe on facing page:

- Divide into 10 pieces and roll into round, slightly flattened buns.

- Place on greased or oiled baking tray. Brush with an egg mixed with a tablespoon of water. Cover with a clean, damp linen teatowel and leave in a warm place until risen.

- Bake as instructed.

- While buns are still warm, drizzle topping mixture over each in the shape of a cross.

66

Hot Cross Buns

Ingredients	Measure	
DOUGH		
Yeast	Teaspoon	$2^1/_2$
Bread Flour	Cup	3
Sugar	Tablespoon	2
Salt	Teaspoon	$^1/_2$
Milk Powder	Tablespoon	2
Butter	Tablespoon	2
Egg (measure with water)		1
Cinnamon	Teaspoon	1
Cloves	Teaspoon	$^1/_2$
Nutmeg	Teaspoon	$^1/_2$
Water	Cup	$1^1/_4$
Raisins	Cup	1
TOPPING		
Icing Sugar	Cup	$^3/_4$
Milk	Tablespoon	1
Almond Essence	Teaspoon	$^1/_4$

- Place first 11 dough ingredients in pan, select Dough cycle and press Start.

- Check liquidity of mixture.

- Place raisins in pan when 'beep' sounds, or 10 minutes from end of final kneading.

- Remove dough at end of cycle and place on lightly floured bench. Cover with a clean, damp cloth and allow to rest for 10 minutes.

- **Follow finishing instructions on facing page.**

- Cook in pre-heated oven at 190°C for 15–20 minutes.

- Remove buns from tray when baked and cool on a rack.

Kamut Bread — Egyptian

Kamut is one of the ancient grains of Egypt. Supposedly enjoyed by Tutenkhamen, today's kamut crops are said to be bred from grains found in a tomb in the 'Valley of the Kings'. If kamut is a close relative of emmer, the ancestor of all modern wheat types, the claim above could very well be right.

The rich nutty flavour and high protein of kamut make it popular with dieticians. Like dinkel or spelt wheat, kamut can be tolerated by some people with wheat allergies.

Kamut Bread — Egyptian

Ingredients	Measure	
Yeast	Teaspoon	2
Kamut Flour	Cup	1
Whole Wheat Flour	Cup	2
Gluten Flour	Tablespoon	2
Honey	Tablespoon	2
Salt	Teaspoon	1
Buttermilk	Cup	1¹/₄

- Place all dough ingredients in pan, select Wholemeal cycle and press Start.

- Check liquidity of mixture.

- Remove bread from pan at end of Bake and cool on a rack.

'Kumminknacke' — Scandinavian Caraway Crispbread

Scandinavians do not use a great variety of spices. Caraway is, however, used frequently for flavouring bread.

To finish recipe on facing page:

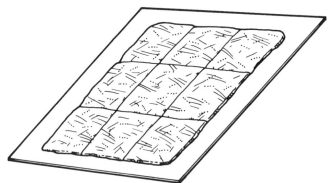

⚜ Divide dough into two pieces.

⚜ Roll each piece out as thinly as possible — the easy way is to roll out dough pieces on buttered baking trays.

⚜ Score dough with knife to mark out crispbread size required. Prick with fork.

⚜ Bake immediately as instructed.

'Kumminknacke' — Scandinavian Caraway Crispbread

Ingredients	Measure	
Yeast	Teaspoon	2
Bread Flour	Cup	1$^1/_2$
Rye Flour	Cup	1$^1/_2$
Sugar	Tablespoon	1
Salt	Teaspoon	$^1/_2$
Milk Powder	Tablespoon	2
Butter	Tablespoon	4
Ground Caraway	Teaspoon	2
Water	Cup	1$^1/_8$
Baking Soda	Teaspoon	1

- Place first nine dough ingredients in pan, select Dough cycle and press Start.

- Check liquidity of mixture.

- Place baking soda in pan when 'beep' sounds, or 10 minutes from end of final kneading.

- Remove dough at end of cycle and place on lightly floured bench. Allow to rest for 10 minutes — no need to cover.

- **Follow finishing instructions on facing page.**

- Cook in pre-heated oven at 225°C for 5–10 minutes until crisp.

- Remove crispbread from trays when baked and cool on a rack.

Laminated Yeast Dough

It has become common to lighten the yeast doughs used for pies, buns and cakes by layering the dough with lard, butter or other fats.

From this has developed such refinements as French croissants, Danish pastries, English lardy cake, Middle Eastern baklava and East European böreks.

Now you could cheat and use ready-made puff or filo pastry from the supermarket. Or you can use one of the laminated yeast dough recipes on **pages 74–75**, to make many of the superb breads in this book.

First Make the basic dough by following the recipe instructions.

Next Create the laminating fat by beating the butter and flour together. Don't overmix, and don't have the mixture softer than the dough. Put it in the refrigerator to keep it under control.

Now

Roll the dough out to a rectangle 2 cm thick.

Cover two-thirds of the dough with all the laminating fat. Leave the remaining third and a margin uncovered.

Fold the uncovered third over the centre third and fold the remaining third over that. Pinch all open edges to seal.

Turn through 90° and roll the dough again to a rectangle. Fold in three as before (no fat this time).

Repeat turning, rolling and folding twice more. The laminated dough is now ready to use. It may be stored covered in the refrigerator.

Laminated Yeast Dough (Plain)

Ingredients	Measure	
DOUGH		
Yeast	Teaspoon	2
Bread Flour	Cup	3
Gluten Flour	Tablespoon	3
Sugar	Tablespoon	3
Salt	Teaspoon	2
Milk Powder	Tablespoon	2
Water	Cup	1¹/₈
LAMINATING FAT		
Butter	Cup	1
Bread Flour	Tablespoon	3

❧ Place all dough ingredients in pan, select Dough cycle and press Start.

❧ Check liquidity of mixture.

❧ Remove dough at end of cycle and place on lightly floured bench. Allow to rest for 10 minutes.

❧ **Follow laminating instructions on pages 72–73.**

Laminated Yeast Dough (Sweet)

Ingredients	Measure	
DOUGH		
Yeast	Teaspoon	4
Bread Flour	Cup	3
Gluten Flour	Tablespoon	3
Sugar	Tablespoon	2
Salt	Teaspoon	1
Butter	Tablespoon	4
Egg (measure with water)		2
Water	Cup	1¹/₈
LAMINATING FAT		
Butter	Cup	2
Bread Flour	Tablespoon	6

🌾 Place all dough ingredients in pan, select Dough cycle and press Start.

🌾 Check liquidity of mixture.

🌾 Remove dough at end of cycle, place on lightly floured bench. Allow to rest for 10 minutes.

🌾 **Follow laminating instructions on pages 72–73.**

Leavened Wheat Loaf — Egyptian

The earliest breads in the Nile Valley were made from barley. This recipe from around 1500 BC probably used emmer wheat, an ancestor of most wheat grown today.

The Egyptian bakers would have placed the dough in a clay pot to prove and cook, much as we use pans when baking bread today. Loaves were not 'slashed' before baking in those days, but you can slash yours if you wish.

Finishing instructions for recipe on facing page:

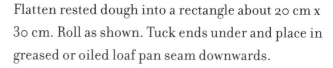

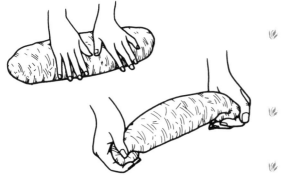

💨 Flatten rested dough into a rectangle about 20 cm x 30 cm. Roll as shown. Tuck ends under and place in greased or oiled loaf pan seam downwards.

💨 Cover with a clean, damp linen teatowel and leave in a warm place to rise to top of pan for 4–5 hours.

💨 Bake as instructed.

Leavened Wheat Loaf — Egyptian

Ingredients	Measure	
Wheat Leaven	Cup	1
Wholemeal Flour	Cup	3
Salt	Teaspoon	$1/4$
Water	Cup	$3/4$

- Place all dough ingredients in pan, select Dough cycle and press Start.

- Check liquidity of mixture.

- Remove dough at end of cycle and place on lightly floured bench. Cover with a clean, damp cloth and allow to rest in a warm place for 60 minutes.

- **Follow finishing instructions on facing page.**

- Cook in pre-heated oven at 200°C for about 60 minutes.

- Remove bread from pan and cool on a rack.

Manchet Bread — English

In fifteenth century England, manchet bread was eaten only by the rich. The flour used was the finest wheat available at the time, milled and sifted to leave only the whitest flour. Made into large rolls (similar in size to baps), manchet was a popular addition to the rich man's table.

Finishing instructions for recipe on facing page:

- Divide rested dough into four. Roll each piece into a ball. Place on greased or oiled baking tray. Press top to flatten slightly.

- Cover with a clean, damp linen teatowel and leave to rise in a warm place for about 30 minutes.

- Place one deep cut in the centre of each loaf to release steam. Brush with milk to glaze.

- Bake as instructed.

Manchet Bread – English

Ingredients	Measure	
DOUGH		
Yeast	Teaspoon	$2^{1}/_{2}$
Bread Flour	Cup	3
Salt	Teaspoon	$^{1}/_{2}$
Butter	Tablespoon	1
Milk Powder	Tablespoon	2
Water	Cup	$1^{1}/_{8}$
GLAZE		
Milk	Tablespoon	2

- Place all dough ingredients in pan, select Dough cycle and press Start.

- Check liquidity of mixture.

- Remove dough at end of cycle and place on lightly floured bench. Cover with a clean, damp cloth and allow to rest in a warm place for 10 minutes.

- **Follow finishing instructions on facing page.**

- Cook in pre-heated oven at 200°C for 20–30 minutes.

- Remove bread from tray when baked and cool on a rack.

Maslin Country Bread — English

This sixteenth century bread, made half from wheat and half from rye flours, would be instantly recognised as 'maslin' by most of the population. The dense chewy loaf was their daily bread. Maslin grain was sometimes grown as a mixed crop and milled as a single grain.

Finishing instructions for recipe on facing page:

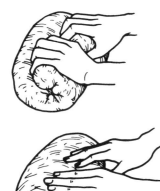

- Flatten rested dough into an oval shape. Roll up as shown to form a cushion shape.

- Place on greased baking tray smooth side up. Cover with a clean, damp linen teatowel and leave to rise in a warm place for about 20 minutes. Slash along top 1 cm deep.

- Brush with milk and sprinkle topping seeds on.

- Bake as instructed.

Slashing the loaf allows steam to escape so the loaf does not burst. It is also used for decoration.

Maslin Country Bread — English

Ingredients	Measure	
SPONGE		
Yeast	Teaspoon	3
Wholemeal Flour	Cup	1¹/₂
Honey	Tablespoon	2
Milk Powder	Tablespoon	4
Water	Cup	1
DOUGH		
Rye Flour	Cup	1¹/₂
Butter	Tablespoon	2
Salt	Teaspoon	¹/₂
TOPPING		
Milk	Tablespoon	1
Poppy Seed	Tablespoon	1

- Place sponge ingredients in pan, select Dough cycle and press Start. After 10 minutes press Stop. Allow to rest for 60 minutes.

- Place remaining dough ingredients in pan with sponge, select Dough cycle again and press Start.

- Check liquidity of mixture.

- Remove dough at end of cycle and place on lightly floured bench. Cover with a clean, damp cloth and allow to rest in a warm place for 40 minutes.

- **Follow finishing instructions on facing page.**

- Cook in pre-heated oven at 180°C for 60 minutes.

- Remove bread from tray when baked and cool on a rack.

Olive Bread — Italian

For the best flavour, serve this bread warm.

In these finishing instructions, onion filling (page 84) is used. You may prefer to substitute your own favourite, or not use a filling at all:

- Divide rested dough into two, shape into balls in floured hands.

- Roll out both balls into flat oval shapes.

- Spread $1/_2$ cup filling (if used) over half of each piece, fold other half over filling and pinch edges to seal.

- Place both pieces on lightly greased or oiled oven tray.

- Brush each with olive oil, spread with a tablespoon of onion topping, and sprinkle with rock salt and rosemary as required.

- Cover with a clean, damp linen teatowel and allow to rise in a warm place for 30–40 minutes.

- Bake as instructed.

Olive Bread — Italian

Ingredients	Measure	
DOUGH		
Yeast	Teaspoon	3
Bread Flour	Cup	3
Salt	Teaspoon	2
Olive Oil	Tablespoon	1
Water	Cup	1¹/₈
Sliced Olives	Cup	¹/₂
TOPPING		
Olive Oil	Teaspoon	2
Onion Filling*	Tablespoon	2
Rock Salt	As required	
Rosemary Leaves	As required	

* See page 84.

🌿 Place first five dough ingredients in pan, select Dough cycle, and press Start.

🌿 Check liquidity of mixture.

🌿 Place sliced olives in pan when 'beep' sounds, or 10 minutes from end of final kneading.

🌿 Remove dough at end of cycle and place on lightly floured bench. Cover with a clean, damp linen teatowel and allow to rest in a warm place for 10 minutes.

🌿 **Follow finishing instructions on facing page.**

🌿 Cook in pre-heated oven at 220°c for 20–25 minutes.

🌿 Remove bread from tray when baked and cool on a rack.

Onion Filling — Italian

Ingredients	Measure	
Olive Oil	Tablespoon	2
Onions	Cup	3
Bay Leaves		2
Rosemary Leaves	Tablespoon	1
Balsamic Vinegar	Tablespoon	2
Brown Sugar	Tablespoon	3
Mustard Seed	Tablespoon	1

Use as requested in recipes!

- Heat oil in a small pan on medium, then add onion, bay leaves and rosemary.

- Reduce to low and brown well, stirring to prevent sticking.

- Add vinegar and stir well.

- Add sugar and mustard seeds, cover and cook over low heat for about 30 minutes, stirring occasionally until thick, brown and shiny. Remove bay leaves.

- Cool completely before using.

- This filling can be stored in an airtight container in the refrigerator for up to three days.

Orange Bread — 'Pan Naranja' — Spanish

Ingredients	Measure	
DOUGH		
Yeast	Teaspoon	2
Bread Flour	Cup	3
Sugar	Tablespoon	2
Salt	Teaspoon	1
Butter	Tablespoon	1
Orange Zest	Tablespoon	$1^1/_2$
Egg (measure with water)		1
Water	Cup	$^7/_8$
Fresh Orange Juice	Cup	$^1/_4$

✺ Place all dough ingredients in pan, select Basic cycle and press Start.

✺ Check liquidity of mixture.

✺ Remove bread from pan at end of Bake and cool on a rack.

Original Spelt Bread

Spelt is one of the oldest cereal grains. Cultivated in Armenia in 5000 BC, it had spread to Syria, Egypt and Ethiopia by 3000 BC and to Europe by 300 BC. Nowadays it is also known by its German name of 'dinkel'.

The mild nutty flavour of spelt has been often praised. The twelfth century Swiss nun, Hildegard of Bingen, wrote that spelt makes its eater 'of joyful mood and happy thoughts'.

Although spelt is a kind of wheat, people with wheat allergies can often tolerate it. Try just a small amount first.

Spelt is grown organically worldwide.

Original Spelt Bread

Ingredients	Measure	
SPONGE		
Yeast	Teaspoon	2
Spelt Flour	Cup	1$^1/_2$
Honey	Tablespoon	$^1/_2$
Water	Cup	$^1/_2$
DOUGH		
Spelt Flour	Cup	1$^1/_2$
Honey	Tablespoon	1
Salt	Teaspoon	1
Water	Cup	$^5/_8$

- Place sponge ingredients in pan, select Dough cycle and press Start. After 10 minutes press Stop. Allow to rest for 2 hours.

- Place remaining dough ingredients in pan with sponge, select French cycle and press Start again.

- Check liquidity of mixture.

- Remove bread from pan at end of Bake and cool on a rack.

Pan de Muerto — Mexican

'Bread of the Dead' — not as sad as it seems at first. The Mexican culture has for many years embraced mortality by paying respects to departed family members at celebrations to remember their passing. This bread is traditionally only made and eaten on All Souls Day — 1 November — a joyous festivity.

Finishing instructions for recipe on facing page:

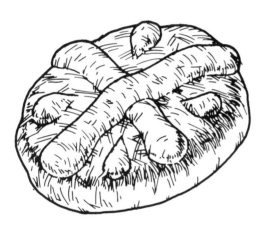

- Divide 'rested' dough into four. Roll three pieces into slightly flattened balls. Divide remaining piece into nine equal parts. Roll six into 12 cm rope, then flatten ends to simulate a bone shape. Divide each of the last three pieces into four equal parts and shape each part into a tear-drop.

- Decorate top of each loaf with two 'bones' and four 'tears' as shown.

- Place on greased or oiled baking tray. Cover with a clean, damp linen teatowel and leave to rise in a warm place for 20–30 minutes.

- Bake as instructed.

- Boil sugar and water until dissolved. When cool, brush on breads and sprinkle with sugar crystals.

Pan de Muerto — Mexican

Ingredients	Measure	
DOUGH		
Yeast	Teaspoon	2¹/₂
Bread Flour	Cup	3
Castor Sugar	Tablespoon	2
Salt	Teaspoon	¹/₂
Butter	Tablespoon	2
Orange Zest	Teaspoon	2
Lemon Zest	Teaspoon	2
Egg (measure with water)		2
Water	Cup	1
TOPPING		
Sugar	Tablespoon	4
Water	Tablespoon	2
Sugar Crystals (coloured)	Tablespoon	3

- Place all dough ingredients in pan, select Dough cycle and press Start.

- Check liquidity of mixture.

- Remove dough at end of cycle and place on lightly floured bench. Cover with a clean, damp linen teatowel and allow to rest in a warm place for 10 minutes.

- Knead in a little more flour if dough becomes sticky after resting.

- **Follow finishing instructions on facing page.**

- Cook in pre-heated oven at 180°C for 30–40 minutes.

- Remove loaves from tray when baked and cool on a rack.

'Birnwähen' — Swiss Pear Bread Pie

This close cousin of the famous Swiss fruit bread 'birnbrot' is an old recipe that was once only made at Christmas. It still is a holiday treat.

Finishing instructions for recipes on page 91 and 92:

- Divide rested dough into two. Roll one piece out to 35 cm diameter, the other to 28 cm diameter.

- Butter a 25 cm diameter deep pie dish and line with largest piece.

- **Add filling from page 92.** Cover with remaining dough piece and moisten and seal edges.

- Cover with a clean, damp linen teatowel and leave to rest in a warm place for 20–30 minutes.

- Mix egg yolk and water glaze and brush on pie top.

- Bake as instructed.

'Birnwähen' — Swiss Pear Bread Pie

Ingredients	Measure	
DOUGH		
Yeast	Teaspoon	2
Bread Flour	Cup	2
Wholemeal Flour	Cup	1
Sugar	Tablespoon	1
Salt	Teaspoon	1
Butter	Tablespoon	2
Egg (measure with water)		1
Milk Powder	Tablespoon	2
Water	Cup	1¹/₈
GLAZE		
Egg Yolk		1
Water	Tablespoon	1

🌿 Place all dough ingredients in pan, select Dough cycle and press Start.

🌿 Check liquidity of mixture.

🌿 Remove dough at end of cycle and place on lightly floured bench. Cover with a clean, damp linen teatowel and allow to rest in a warm place for 10 minutes.

🌿 **Follow finishing instructions on facing page.**

🌿 Cook in pre-heated oven at 180°c for about 30–40 minutes.

🌿 Remove from dish as soon as possible when baked. Cool on a rack.

'Birnwähen' — Swiss Pear Bread Pie

Ingredients	Measure	
FILLING		
Chopped Dried Pears	Cup	2
Chopped Pitted Prunes	Cup	$^1/_2$
Raisins	Cup	$^1/_2$
Sultanas	Cup	$^1/_2$
Chopped Candied Peel	Cup	$^1/_2$
Lemon Zest	Teaspoon	2
Brandy	Cup	$^1/_4$
Red Wine (Merlot)	Cup	1
Water	As required	
Nutmeg	Teaspoon	$^1/_4$
Coriander	Teaspoon	$^1/_4$
Cinnamon	Teaspoon	$^1/_2$
Chopped Almonds	Tablespoon	1
Chopped Walnuts	Tablespoon	2
Pine Nuts	Tablespoon	1

To use this filling, follow finishing instructions on page 90.

- Place first eight ingredients in a covered pan and leave overnight.

- Add enough water to raise liquid level to two-thirds up fruit.

- Boil, then simmer, stirring often, to reduce liquid. Continue until fruit is a moist mash.

- When cool, stir in all the remaining ingredients.

Kulich — Russian Easter Bread

Ingredients	Measure	
DOUGH		
Yeast	Teaspoon	$2^1/_2$
Bread Flour	Cup	3
Castor Sugar	Tablespoon	2
Salt	Teaspoon	$^1/_4$
Cinnamon	Teaspoon	1
Mixed Peel	Cup	$^1/_4$
Milk Powder	Tablespoon	2
Butter	Tablespoon	3
Egg (measure with water)		1
Water	Cup	$1^1/_8$
Raisins	Cup	$^1/_2$
Chopped Almonds	Cup	$^1/_4$
GLAZE		
Icing Sugar	Cup	1
Lemon Juice	Tablespoon	1

- Place first 10 dough ingredients in pan, select Basic cycle and press Start.

- Check liquidity of mixture.

- Place remaining dough ingredients in pan when 'beep' sounds, or 10 minutes from end of final kneading.

- Remove bread from pan at end of Bake and cool on a rack.

- Mix glaze and drizzle on when bread is cool.

Pirozhki (Little Pies) — Russian

Russian cooks over the years have perfected using yeast dough for the great variety of breads, pies and pancakes they eat on all occasions. Pirozhki are small pies or turnovers baked (as here) or deep fried. The range of fillings is huge and some samples appear on the following pages.

Finishing instructions for recipe on facing page, with fillings on pages 96 and 97:

- Roll out rested dough to about 3 mm thick. Cut out 7–8 cm diameter pieces with pastry cutter.

- Put chosen filling in centre of each piece (about 2 tablespoons).

- Fold in two, moisten and seal edges. Place on greased baking sheet. Brush with topping.

- Cover with a clean, damp linen teatowel and leave to rise in a warm place for 15–30 minutes.

- Bake as instructed.

Pirozhki (Little Pies) — Russian

Ingredients	Measure	
DOUGH		
Yeast	Teaspoon	2^1/$_2$
Bread Flour	Cup	3
Sugar	Tablespoon	2
Salt	Teaspoon	^{1}/$_2$
Butter	Tablespoon	2
Milk Powder	Tablespoon	4
Egg (measure with water)		2
Water	Cup	1^1/$_8$
TOPPING		
Egg (beaten with water)		1
Water	Tablespoon	2

🌿 Place all dough ingredients in pan, select Dough cycle and press Start.

🌿 Check liquidity of mixture.

🌿 Remove dough at end of cycle and place on lightly floured bench. Cover with a clean, damp teatowel and allow to rest in a warm place for 10 minutes.

🌿 **Follow finishing instructions on facing page.**

🌿 Cook in pre-heated oven at 180°C for about 15 minutes until golden.

🌿 Remove pirozhki from sheet when baked and cool on a rack.

Pirozhki — Fillings

Ingredients	Measure		
Cabbage			
Shredded Cooked Cabbage	Cup	1	
Cooked Rice	Cup	1	✍ Mix all together.
Sultanas	Cup	$1/2$	
Potato			
Boiled Potato	Cup	2	✍ Drain and mash potatoes.
Butter	Tablespoon	2	✍ Beat with butter.
Black pepper to taste			✍ Add pepper.
Apple			
Stewed Apple	Cup	1	✍ Drain all excess moisture from apple in a strainer.
Cottage Cheese	Cup	1	✍ Drain all excess moisture from cheese in a strainer.
Raisins	Cup	$1/4$	✍ Mix well with raisins.
Sugar	To taste		✍ Add sugar.
Beef			
Minced Beef	Cup	1	✍ Fry beef in butter until cooked.
Butter	Tablespoon	2	✍ Add onion.
Chopped Onion	Cup	1	✍ Mix well.
Egg, hard-boiled and chopped		2	✍ Place in bowl with egg.

Pirozhki — Fillings

Ingredients	Measure		
Buckwheat			
Chopped Onion	Cup	1	Fry onions in butter until soft.
Butter	Tablespoon	2	Add buckwheat.
Cooked Buckwheat	Cup	1	Mix well.
Egg, hard-boiled and chopped		2	Place in bowl with egg.
Mushroom			
Sliced Mushroom	Cup	$1^1/_2$	Cook mushrooms in butter until tender.
Butter	Tablespoon	2	Add sour cream, simmer 10–15 mins, cool.
Chopped Onion	Cup	$^1/_2$	Add onion.
Sour Cream	Cup	$^1/_4$	Mix well.
Egg			
Egg, beaten		3	Beat all together until creamy.
Cottage Cheese	Cup	$1^1/_2$	Drain cottage cheese in a strainer.
Butter	Tablespoon	1	

Plain Bread 'Pain Ordinaire' — French

These are the 'twice a day — everyday' baguettes produced by craftsman bakers throughout France. The Parisians call them 'bâtards' because they love to be different! The ingredients used, and the availability twice daily of the finished product, have been prescribed by law since the Revolution.

Finishing instructions for recipe on facing page:

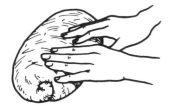

- Divide rested dough into two. Shape each into a ball. Press each ball into a 20 cm x 20 cm square. Fold over and roll up (see illustration). Cover with a clean, damp linen teatowel and rest with seam downwards in a warm place while you shape the other piece.

- Gently roll each piece into a 30 cm long loaf. Place on greased baking sheet. Cover as before and leave to rise in a warm place for about 90 minutes.

- Slash three or four diagonal cuts across each loaf.

- Brush with water.

- Bake as instructed.

Plain Bread 'Pain Ordinaire' — French

Ingredients	Measure	
SPONGE		
Yeast	Teaspoon	2$\frac{1}{2}$
Bread Flour	Cup	1$\frac{1}{2}$
Water	Cup	1
DOUGH		
Bread Flour	Cup	1$\frac{1}{2}$
Salt	Teaspoon	1
Water	Cup	$\frac{1}{4}$

🌾 Place sponge ingredients in pan, select Dough cycle and press Start. After 10 minutes press Stop. Allow to rest for 4 hours in pan until doubled in size.

🌾 Place remaining dough ingredients in pan with sponge, select Dough cycle again and press Start.

🌾 Check liquidity of mixture.

🌾 Remove dough at end of cycle and place on lightly floured bench. Cover with a clean, damp linen teatowel and allow to rest in a warm place for 10 minutes.

🌾 **Follow finishing instructions on facing page.**

🌾 Cook in pre-heated oven at 230°C for 20–30 minutes.

🌾 Remove baguettes from sheet when baked and cool on a rack.

Plain Bread 'Pain Ordinaire' — French Machine Version

Ingredients	Measure	
Yeast	Teaspoon	2
Bread Flour	Cup	3
Sugar	Tablespoon	1^1/$_2$
Salt	Teaspoon	1
Butter	Tablespoon	1^1/$_2$

- Place all dough ingredients in pan, select Basic cycle and press Start.

- Check liquidity of mixture.

- Remove bread from pan at end of Bake and cool on a rack.

Rye Bread — Latvian

Ingredients	Measure	
Yeast	Teaspoon	2
Bread Flour	Cup	2
Rye Flour	Cup	1
Sugar	Teaspoon	1
Salt	Teaspoon	1
Honey	Tablespoon	2
Butter	Tablespoon	2
Caraway Seed	Teaspoon	$1/2$
Water	Cup	$1^1/_8$

🌾 Place all dough ingredients in pan. Set Dark Crust, then Wholewheat cycle and press Start. Some breadmakers do not allow both Dark Crust and Wholewheat. For these, select Wholewheat.

🌾 Check liquidity of mixture.

🌾 Remove bread from pan at end of Bake and cool on a rack.

Rye Sourdough — USA

Rye bread taken to America by immigrants from Central and Eastern Europe is now an established favourite in America. This sourdough version is one of the most popular.

Finishing instructions for recipe on facing page:

- Roll rested dough into a smooth ball by tucking all loose ends underneath. Place on greased or oiled baking tray and slightly flatten top. Cover with a clean, damp linen teatowel and leave to rise in a warm place.

- Slash top with chequer pattern about 1 cm deep. The deeper the cut, the chunkier the crust. Brush with water.

- Bake as directed.

Rye Sourdough — USA

Ingredients	Measure	
SPONGE		
Sourdough Starter	Cup	$^1/_2$
Wholemeal Flour	Cup	$1^1/_2$
Water	Cup	1
DOUGH		
Rye Flour	Cup	1
Wholemeal	Cup	$^1/_2$
Oil	Tablespoon	2
Salt	Teaspoon	1

- Place sponge ingredients in pan, select Dough cycle and press Start. After 10 minutes press Stop. Allow to rest for 12 hours.

- Replace $^1/_2$ cup starter (**see page 7**).

- Place remaining dough ingredients in pan, select Dough cycle again and press Start.

- Check liquidity of mixture.

- Remove dough at end of cycle and place on lightly floured bench. Cover with a clean, damp linen teatowel and allow to rest in a warm place for 10 minutes.

- **Follow finishing instructions on facing page**.

- Cook in pre-heated oven at 210°C for 55–60 minutes.

- Remove loaf from tray when baked and cool on a rack.

Rye, Spelt and Caraway Loaf

Although spelt is rightfully called an 'ancient' grain, it is admirably suited to modern technology, as both this and the previous recipe demonstrate.

The two spelt recipes in this book have both been adapted for the bread machine from the ancient originals.

If caraway is not for you, feel free to experiment with your choice of spice.

Rye, Spelt and Caraway Loaf

Ingredients	Measure	
Yeast	Teaspoon	3
Spelt Flour	Cup	1¹/₂
Rye Flour	Cup	1¹/₂
Gluten Flour	Tablespoon	1
Honey	Tablespoon	1¹/₂
Salt	Teaspoon	1
Butter	Tablespoon	2
Caraway Seed	Teaspoon	2
Water	Cup	1¹/₈

🌾 Place all dough ingredients in pan, select Wholemeal cycle and press Start.

🌾 Check liquidity of mixture.

🌾 Remove bread from pan at end of Bake and cool on a rack.

Spiced Semolina Loaf

Another of the vast number of spicy breads from the Middle East and North Africa.

This tasty loaf is Algerian in origin.

It is quite dense and chewy. Try it with soup.

Spiced Semolina Loaf

Ingredients	Measure	
Yeast	Teaspoon	2
Fine Semolina Flour	Cup	3
Sugar	Teaspoon	$^1/_2$
Ground Cinnamon	Teaspoon	2
Caraway Seed	Tablespoon	1
Sesame Seed	Tablespoon	2
Butter	Tablespoon	$1^1/_2$
Egg (measure with water)		1
Oil	Tablespoon	2
Water	Cup	$1^1/_8$

- Place all dough ingredients in pan, select Wholemeal cycle and press Start.

- Check liquidity of mixture.

- Remove bread from pan at end of Bake and cool on a rack.

Saint Lucia Bread — Swedish

In Sweden, 13 December is celebrated as Saint Lucia's Day. Saint Lucia, known as the Queen of Lights, was a Christian martyr who died in 303 AD. In her memory and on her day, young Swedish girls serve these saffron breads to their families.

You may, if you wish, drizzle a mix of icing sugar and water on the cooled bread and sprinkle sliced almonds or raisins over the top.

Saint Lucia Bread — Swedish

Ingredients	Measure	
DOUGH		
Saffron	Teaspoon	1
Water (boiling)	Cup	¹/₄
Yeast	Teaspoon	2
Wholemeal Flour	Cup	1
Bread Flour	Cup	2
Sugar	Tablespoon	3
Salt	Teaspoon	1
Milk Powder	Tablespoon	3
Oil	Tablespoon	2
Egg (measure with water)		1
Water	Cup	1
TOPPING		
Egg		1
Water	Tablespoon	1

- Combine first two ingredients and allow to cool.

- Place remaining dough ingredients in pan in order recommended in your machine instruction book. Add saffron wash last.

- Select Dough cycle, press Start.

- Remove dough at end of cycle and place on lightly floured bench. Cover with a clean, damp linen teatowel and allow to rest in a warm place for 10 minutes.

- Divide into 10 pieces, roll each piece 25 cm long, curl to form S shape and place on greased or oiled baking tray. Cover as before and leave until doubled in volume (20–30 minutes).

- Coat with egg and water mixture topping.

- Place in pre-heated oven at 200°C for 15 minutes.

- Remove bread from tray when baked and cool on a rack.

Tahini Rolls — 'Tahinov Gata' — Armenian

These deliciously unusual rolls are made mostly for special celebrations, but you can enjoy them any time.

Finishing instructions for recipe on facing page:

- Divide rested dough into six pieces. Roll each into a ball, then flatten each ball into a circle as thin as possible. Spread each with an equal share of tahini and brown sugar. Roll each piece up Swiss roll fashion.

- Place on buttered baking tray. Cover with a clean, damp linen teatowel and leave to rise in a warm place for 30 minutes.

- Brush with mixed egg and milk glaze.

- Bake as instructed.

Tahini Rolls — 'Tahinov Gata' — Armenian

Ingredients	Measure	
DOUGH		
Yeast	Teaspoon	2
Bread Flour	Cup	3
Sugar	Tablespoon	2
Salt	Teaspoon	$^1/_2$
Butter	Tablespoon	6
Egg (measure with water)		1
Milk Powder	Tablespoon	2
Water	Cup	$1^1/_8$
FILLING		
Tahini	Cup	1
Brown Sugar	Cup	$^3/_4$
GLAZE		
Egg		1
Milk	Teaspoon	1

❧ Place all dough ingredients in pan, select Dough cycle and press Start.

❧ Check liquidity of mixture.

❧ Remove dough at end of cycle and place on lightly floured bench. Cover with a clean, damp linen teatowel and allow to rest in a warm place for 10 minutes.

❧ **Follow finishing instructions on facing page.**

❧ Cook in pre-heated oven at 190°C for 30–40 minutes until golden.

❧ Remove rolls from tray when baked and cool on a rack.

Trencher Bread — English

In medieval England, trenchers were 'plates' of four-day-old flat bread off which the meal was eaten. The 'plates' were made by slicing the loaf horizontally. The top slice always went to the most important guest — hence 'the upper crust'. Even today, a person who clears their plate is 'a good trencherman'.

In 1387 King Richard II gave a banquet where over one thousand loaves were sliced up for trenchers. By 1650 wood or earthenware plates were mostly in use, but some people still prepared trenchers, perhaps because they also liked to eat the plate! It was more usual, though, for 'used' trenchers to be given to the poor and needy to eat.

Finishing instructions for recipe on facing page:

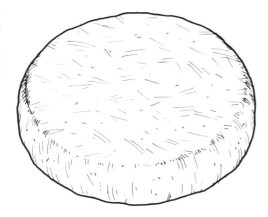

- Divide dough into two equal pieces and roll into balls.

- Roll balls out to form two flat circles about 20 cm diameter.

- Place on greased or oiled baking tray. Cover with a clean, damp linen teatowel and leave to rise in a warm place until doubled in volume.

- Bake as directed.

- Use when four days old.

Trencher Bread — English

Ingredients	Measure	
SPONGE		
Wholemeal Leaven	Cup	1
Wholemeal Flour	Cup	1¹/₂
Water	Cup	³/₄
DOUGH		
Barleymeal (fine)	Cup	1
Salt	Teaspoon	¹/₂

〰 Place sponge ingredients in pan, select Dough cycle and press Start. After 10 minutes press Stop. Allow to rest for six hours.

〰 Place remaining dough ingredients in pan with rested sponge. Select Dough cycle and press Start.

〰 Check liquidity of mixture.

〰 Remove dough at end of cycle and place on lightly floured bench. Cover with a clean, damp linen teatowel and allow to rest in a warm place for 10 minutes.

〰 **Follow finishing instructions on facing page.**

〰 Cook in pre-heated oven at 210°C for 50 minutes.

〰 Remove bread from tray when baked and cool on a rack.

Welsh Crumpets — Original

Crumpets are known all over the world as a 'must' for the English afternoon tea. Different recipes are found all over England. This version from the neighbouring Welsh principality produces something more likc a griddle cake or pikelets.

Finishing instructions for recipe on facing page:

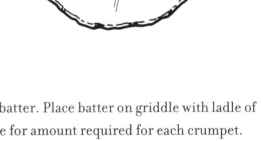

🌾 Stir to mix batter. Place batter on griddle with ladle of suitable size for amount required for each crumpet. Place two or three at a time, depending on griddle size.

🌾 Cook as instructed.

Eat Welsh crumpets with butter, honey or cream.

Welsh Crumpets — Original

Ingredients	Measure	
Yeast	Teaspoon	3
Bread Flour	Cup	3
Salt	Teaspoon	1
Butter	Tablespoon	2
Egg (measure with water)		2
Milk Powder	Tablespoon	2
Water	Cup	2

- Place all dough ingredients in pan, select Dough cycle and press Start.

- Check liquidity of mixture — it should be like a thick pancake batter.

- Remove batter at end of cycle, place in a bowl, cover with a clean, damp linen teatowel and allow to rest for 60 minutes.

- **Follow finishing instructions on facing page.**

- Cook on pre-heated griddle at 175°C for 2–3 minutes each side.

- Remove cooked crumpets to dish in heated oven to keep warm. Cover dish with a clean, dry linen teatowel.

White Bloomer Sourdough — English

Many English bakers still use the sourdough starter. The starter is sometimes called 'old dough' and is used to create an active sponge in the usual manner. Some French bakers, who also use the same starter, are said to call it a 'poolish' — but that doesn't look very French to me!

Finishing instructions for recipe on facing page:

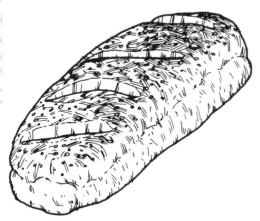

- Shape rested dough into a ball.

- Press into a 25 cm x 30 cm rectangle. Roll up to form a cushion shape.

- Gently roll into a 35 cm long loaf.

- Place on a greased baking tray. Cover and leave in a warm place to rise.

- Slash with cuts, as shown.

- Brush on water and sprinkle with poppy seeds.

- Bake as instructed.

White Bloomer Sourdough — English

Ingredients	Measure		
SPONGE			
Sourdough Starter	Cup		$^1/_2$
Bread Flour	Cup		$1^1/_2$
Water	Cup		1
DOUGH			
Bread Flour	Cup		$1^1/_2$
Oil	Tablespoon		1
Salt	Teaspoon		$^1/_2$
TOPPING			
Water	Tablespoon		1
Poppy Seed	Tablespoon		1

- Place sponge ingredients in pan, select Dough cycle and press Start. After 10 minutes press Stop. Allow to rest eight hours.

- Replace $^1/_2$ cup starter (**see page 7**).

- Place remaining dough ingredients in pan with sponge, select Dough cycle again and press Start.

- Check liquidity of mixture.

- Remove dough at end of cycle and place on lightly floured bench. Cover with a clean, damp linen teatowel and allow to rest in a warm place for 10 minutes.

- **Follow finishing instructions on facing page.**

- Cook in pre-heated oven at 200°C for 45–55 minutes.

- Remove loaf from tray when baked and cool on a rack.

White Bread Plait 'Zopf' — Swiss

In Switzerland 'zopf' means 'plait'. Therefore a zopf is always a plump, golden, plaited loaf of white dough enriched with the eggs and milk the country is famous for. Always a 'Sunday' bread for high day and holidays.

Finishing instructions for recipe on facing page:

- Divide rested dough into three. Roll each piece into a 30 cm long sausage shape.

- Plait the pieces together as shown and tuck ends under. Place on a greased or oiled baking tray.

- Brush with egg yolk and water beaten together to glaze.

- Cover with a clean, damp linen teatowel and leave in a warm place until well risen for about 60 minutes.

- Bake as instructed.

White Bread Plait 'Zopf' — Swiss

Ingredients	Measure	
DOUGH		
Yeast	Teaspoon	2¹/₂
Bread Flour	Cup	3
Sugar	Teaspoon	1
Salt	Teaspoon	1
Butter	Tablespoon	2
Egg (measure with water)		1
Milk Powder	Tablespoon	2
Water	Cup	1¹/₈
GLAZE		
Egg Yolk		1
Water	Tablespoon	1

- Place all dough ingredients in pan, select Dough cycle and press Start.

- Check liquidity of mixture.

- Remove dough at end of cycle and place on lightly floured bench. Cover with a clean, damp linen teatowel and allow to rest in a warm place for 10 minutes.

- **Follow finishing instructions on facing page.**

- Cook in pre-heated oven at 200°C for about 30 minutes.

- Remove loaf from tray when baked and cool on a rack.

Wholemeal Sourdough — USA

The pioneers moving westwards in America carried with them their own leaven saved from one day to the next to activate their bread dough. This gave their bread the tangy sour flavour they enjoyed. No sourdough is better than that made in San Francisco where a local airborne bacillus gives the dough an extra kick.

Finishing instructions for recipe on facing page:

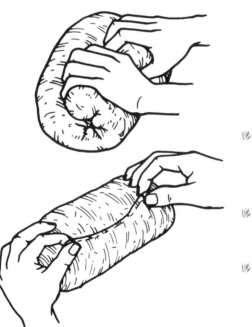

- Flatten rested dough into a rectangle about 20 cm x 30 cm. Roll as shown. Tuck ends under and place in greased loaf pan seam downwards.

- Cover with a clean, damp linen teatowel and leave in a warm place to rise to top of pan. Slash top of loaf.

- Bake as instructed.

Wholemeal Sourdough — USA

Ingredients	Measure	
SPONGE		
Sourdough Starter	Cup	¹/₂
Wholemeal Flour	Cup	1¹/₂
Water	Cup	1¹/₈
DOUGH		
Wholemeal Flour	Cup	1¹/₂
Oil	Tablespoon	1
Salt	Teaspoon	1

- Place sponge ingredients in pan, select Dough cycle and press Start. After 10 minutes press Stop. Allow to rest for 12 hours.

- Replace ¹/₂ cup of starter (**see page 7**).

- Place remaining dough ingredients in pan, select Dough cycle again and press Start.

- Check liquidity of mixture.

- Remove dough at end of cycle and place on lightly floured bench. Cover with a clean, damp linen teatowel and allow to rise in a warm place for 10 minutes.

- **Follow finishing instructions on facing page.**

- Cook in pre-heated oven at 210°C for 55–65 minutes.

- Remove loaf from pan when baked and cool on a rack.

Wholemeal Wheat (Leavened) — East Anglian

During the Roman period of Britain (55BC–450AD), the area now known as East Anglia produced vast quantities of high-quality wheat. Towards the end of the period, more and more wheat was exported to Rome. The Roman soldiers objected that, having lost their good wheat bread, they were forced to eat bread made from barley (**see page 30**). This bread is still made with a leaven by many bakers who shun commercial yeasts.

Finishing instructions for recipe on facing page:

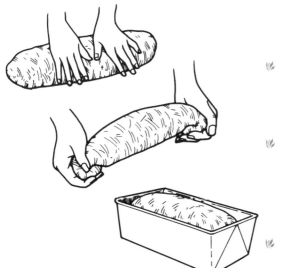

- Flatten rested dough into a rectangle approximately 20 cm x 30 cm. Roll as shown, tuck ends under and place in greased or oiled loaf pan, seam downwards.

- Cover with a clean, damp linen teatowel and leave in a warm place for about 4 hours to rise to top of tin. Slash top of loaf with three (the traditional number!) diagonals.

- Bake as instructed.

122

Wholemeal Wheat (Leavened) — East Anglian

Ingredients	Measure	
Wheat Leaven	Cup	$1^1/_2$
Wholemeal Flour	Cup	$2^1/_4$
Honey	Tablespoon	1
Salt	Teaspoon	$^1/_4$
Water	Cup	$^3/_4$

- Replace leaven used with same quantity of fresh flour and water.

- Place all dough ingredients in pan, select Dough cycle and press Start.

- Check liquidity of mixture.

- Remove dough at end of cycle and place on lightly floured bench. Cover with a clean, damp linen teatowel and allow to rest in a warm place for 10 minutes.

- **Follow finishing instructions on facing page.**

- Cook in pre-heated oven at 205°C for about 60 minutes.

- Remove loaf from pan when baked and cool on a rack.

Table 1 Equivalent measures for parts of cups and spoons

1 Cup	= 16	Tablespoons	= 48	Teaspoons
$^7/_8$ Cup	= 14	Tablespoons	= 42	Teaspoons
$^3/_4$ Cup	= 12	Tablespoons	= 36	Teaspoons
$^5/_8$ Cup	= 10	Tablespoons	= 30	Teaspoons
$^1/_2$ Cup	= 8	Tablespoons	= 24	Teaspoons
$^3/_8$ Cup	= 6	Tablespoons	= 18	Teaspoons
$^1/_4$ Cup	= 4	Tablespoons	= 12	Teaspoons
$^1/_8$ Cup	= 2	Tablespoons	= 6	Teaspoons

1 Tablespoon	= 3	Teaspoons
$^7/_8$ Tablespoon	= $2^1/_2$	Teaspoons
$^3/_4$ Tablespoon	= 2	Teaspoons
$^5/_8$ Tablespoon	= $1^3/_4$	Teaspoons
$^1/_2$ Tablespoon	= $1^1/_2$	Teaspoons
$^3/_8$ Tablespoon	= 1	Teaspoon
$^1/_4$ Tablespoon	= $^3/_4$	Teaspoon
$^1/_8$ Tablespoon	= $^1/_2$	Teaspoon

- All above to nearest logical amount.
- Your cup measure should be 250 ml capacity and graduated in $^1/_8$ cup steps.
- Your spoon set should contain:

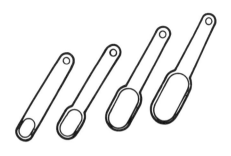

1	15 ml	tablespoon
1	5 ml	teaspoon
1	2.5 ml	$^1/_2$ teaspoon
1	1.25 ml	$^1/_4$ teaspoon

Description	Fahrenheit °F	Celsius °C	Gas Mark
Cool	225	110	$^1/_4$
	250	130	$^1/_2$
Very Slow	275	140	1
	300	150	2
Slow	325	170	3
Moderate	350	180	4
	375	190	5
Moderately Hot	400	200	6
Fairly Hot	425	220	7
Hot	450	230	8
Very Hot	475	240	9
Extremely Hot	500	250	10

Table 3 Volume conversions to nearest logical amount

Fluid oz.	Pint	Millilitre	Litre	Teaspoon	NZ Tablespoon	Cup	Aust. Tablespoon
		5		1			
		10		2			
		15		3	1	$^1/_{16}$	
		20		4			1
1		25		5			
	$^1/_{16}$	30			2	$^1/_8$	
		40		8			2
		45		9	3		
2		50		10			
	$^1/_8$	60		12	4	$^1/_4$	3
3		75			5		
		80		16			4
		85				$^1/_3$ *	
	$^3/_{16}$	90			6	$^3/_8$	
4		100		20			5
5	$^1/_4$	125	$^1/_8$		8	$^1/_2$	6
6		150					
		155			10	$^5/_8$	
		170			11	$^2/_3$ **	
	$^3/_8$	185			12	$^3/_4$	

Fluid oz.	Pint	Millilitre	Litre	Teaspoon	NZ Tablespoon	Cup	Aust. Tablespoon
8		200		40	13		10
		220			14	$^7/_8$	
10	$^1/_2$	250	$^1/_4$		16	1	12
		280			18	$1^1/_8$	
12		300		60			15
	$^5/_8$	310			20	$1^1/_4$	
14		350					
15	$^3/_4$	375	$^3/_8$		24	$1^1/_2$	
	$^7/_8$	440			28	$1^3/_4$	
20	1	500	$^1/_2$		32	2	25
30	$1^1/_2$	750	$^3/_4$		48	3	
40	2	1,000	1			4	50

* Equals $^3/_8$ cup less 1 teaspoon

** Equals $^5/_8$ cup plus 1 tablespoon

Table 4 Conversion of recipe quantities to other machine sizes

Use for either cup or tablespoon or teaspoon metric measures.

MACHINE SIZES

1 lb	1^1/$_2$ lb	2 lb	2^1/$_2$ lb		
^{1}/$_8$	^{3}/$_{16}$	^{1}/$_4$	^{5}/$_{16}$		
^{1}/$_4$	^{3}/$_8$	^{1}/$_2$	^{5}/$_8$		
^{3}/$_8$	^{1}/$_2$	^{3}/$_4$	^{7}/$_8$		
^{1}/$_2$	^{3}/$_4$	1	1^1/$_4$		
^{5}/$_8$	1	1^1/$_4$	1^5/$_8$		
^{3}/$_4$	1^1/$_8$	1^1/$_2$	1^7/$_8$		
^{7}/$_8$	1^3/$_8$	1^3/$_4$	2^1/$_4$		
1	1^1/$_2$	2	2^1/$_2$		

MACHINE SIZES

1 lb	1½ lb	2 lb	2½ lb
1⅛	1¾	2¼	2⅞
1¼	1⅞	2½	3⅛
1⅜	2	2¾	3⅜
1½	2¼	3	3¾
1⅝	2½	3¼	4⅛
1¾	2⅝	3½	4⅜
1⅞	2¾	3¾	4⅝
2	3	4	5

🌿 All to nearest logical amount.

To convert a recipe from the recipe size to another, find the ingredient quantity in this book's recipe size (1½ lb column) — and read off the size you require on the same line, using the same cup, tablespoon, or teaspoon measure.

HELP!

You are having problems with your machine malfunctioning and don't know where to go for parts or service in your area?

Or you are having trouble in finding a supplier for certain ingredients?

Or you just can't get the right result from a recipe you want to impress everybody with?

Call for Help!

Telephone (or fax) the 'Daley Bread' message centre at Wellington on (04) 589 4094 (listen to the instructions).

Or write to 'Daley Bread' at PO Box 38020, Wellington Mail Centre.

Advice is free (apart from your call cost, postage, or fax to me).

Whether you phone, write or fax, don't forget your name, address and phone number, and the details of your breadmaker.

And if you have a breadmaking experience to relate, or an original recipe you would like to pass on, please write to me at 'Daley Bread', as above. (A letter is best — as long as you like — and it costs less.)

Happy breadmaking!

George Dale

Index